Hurting and Crying Out

Hurting and Crying Out

Sandy Hardy

Contents

My hope in writing this book is that we can make a difference. You are loved and chosen by God, with hope and a future. You are loved, certainly God's love which is pure- and his plans for your life-outweighs anything against you.

Please know you are important, and you CAN achieve.

You can overcome.

There's nothing or anyone so adverse or materially important to ever waste or think about taking your life.

Medically, financially, relationship, nothing.

You are wanted.

You are loved.

By far and by all means, seek, reach out, call out, shout out for assistance, counseling, medical treatment. First and foremost, know Jesus as your savior.

Know without a shadow of doubt, God, loves you unconditionally., he will never leave or forsake you.

God is the healer.

There are some beautiful Christian retreats, and non-Christian, but they are available to relax, recoup, and be there for you.

There are also recovery options that assist and aid in giving you medical care.

Seek God in all things.

Health, relationships, finances, lack, contrite spirit-feelings-angst.

Know, that God has this.

God is for you.

If God be for you who dare go against you!

Compassion, let it move you. To love, to love yourself- to be able to love others.

Forgiveness-not unto what someone has done- not to you are entitled- not to the hurt- abuse- lack- or pain inflicted- or illness-addictions-

Whatever the case may be-

When you can't God can.

Always!

Balance yourself, your thoughts- conditions over and totally into his hands.

God is joy.

God is peace.

God is love.

Don't quit

Don't give up hope!

You are loved.

When you are feeling lost, and with no hope, turn and pray.

Reach out.

Stand and Shout!

Call the crisis center, a friend, family, no matter-

Stand and Shout!

You <u>do</u> matter- you are loved- you are precious- you are wanted.

You are the son/daughter of Christ!

You are my sister, my brother!

There are books (a few) by several authors and one you may want to read.

There are retreats mentioned above and recovery.

Check in your area but do the research.

Hurting and Crying Out

There are physicians, psychologists, specialists, that can diagnose and treat.

Again, check in your area.

In an emergency call your emergency crisis number.

Call family and friends. Even 911.

Reach out- stand and shout out-

Reach for God-

Pray-

Put all your cares into God's hands.

May the good Lord's love comfort you and keep you.

Much love and success always!

Introduction

There are many precious lives (people) out there that we have lost to suicide. It has become an epidemic of proportions.

From many stars, prominent to every individual.

The loss is the same- a loved one, someone special and loved. Matters nothing composing or attaching a status. (A title on them).

We are all children of God. And belong to one family.

The Kingdom of God.

As God's family, we need to show our compassion to everyone.

Never losing hope or sight as to what God, can do.

Looking at today and feeling angst, there is-

The answer-

The answer in all things is to surrender yourself to God and know Jesus as your personal savior.

That no matter what you are facing-

Christ has overcome!

Christ faced temptation.

God, knows all, sees all, and loves each one of us, unconditionally.

The walls, blocks, conditions, you are facing can change, when you rest in God as your father.

You walk by faith not by sight.

Believe in God with your whole heart-

Take hold of his hand and let him be your divine compass.

There is nothing difficult with God.

His will (God's) be done.

Hurting and Crying Out

Say to that (Mountain) enemy, go into the sea – casting and believing.

For each step taken is a step towards his promises.

No matter what opposition you are facing, God, is the answer.

That tomorrow you have hoped for is today-Right now!

God can change everything.

Counseling is available for the lost and hurting- seek God's hand in the direction you would like to take.

Chapter 1

Though I might appear to look alright on the outside, my soul is crying out on the inside. Do you know me? I am the tormentor.

Stand strong and flee from within me.

James 4-7 KJV Submit yourselves therefore to God. Resist the devil, and he will flee from you.

I am no different from you and you are no different from me. We are all equal in the things that we go through. The travails that occur may be different, however the way we are to respond is in the honoring and the obedience of Christ. God's word. Trials and sufferings. We have the savior and king of kings at our side. We can take refuge under his mighty wings and stand strong when the battle is on. God is our comforter.

Deuteronomy 27-10 KJV Thou shalt therefore obey the voice of the Lord thy God and do his commandments and his statues, which I command thee this day.

Revelation 19-16 KJV And he hath on his vesture and on his thigh a name written. King of Kings and Lord of Lords.

Psalm 91-4 KJV He shall cover thee with his feathers, and under his wings shall thou trust his truth shall be thy shield and buckler.

You may feel as if everything is coming on strong and there is no outlet. Know that whatever comes against you, God gives you the strength to stand against it and fight. It is his hand of power. If God is there for you, who dare come against you? Affirm this and meditate on it. Nothing coming against you or happening to you is to great for our father. God our Father, today, tomorrow and infinitely. Allow that to resonate inside and firmly grasp onto it and feel the encompassing love of our Father. You will see that the proper response to the situation soon departs, and calm and peace appear. Grasp it. Hold on dearly to it.

Hebrews 13-6 KJV So that we may boldly say the Lord is my helper, and I will not fear what man shall do unto me.

Isaiah 40-31 KJV But they that wait upon the Lord shall renew their strength, they shall mount up with wings as eagles, they shall run, and not be weary, and they shall walk, and not faint.

When you say you do not understand what I am going through, and nobody does, you are trying to enable someone and manipulate them. For crying out on the inside is a deep hurt and groan. It is the spirit crying out to you to reach out to him. To wrap your arms around him and welcome him into your heart. Where he can guide you and lead you. It hurts, yes, it hurts deeply, but there is nothing or no one or anything in and on the earth, worth checking out over!! God says come to me who are weary and I, I, God will give you rest. The circumstances are not what they appear, and your reaction to the circumstances is what makes them appear bad. Your over-inflated idea of something worse, when in all actuality the trust you are supposed to have with and in God, you are doubting. God says I will never leave or forsake you, and he has not ever left you. That deep feeling of hurt and no answer or response to it is something that only God can answer and handle. He knew you before you were born. You are wonderfully and uniquely made. Designed by the Master.

Psalm 139 14 KJV I will praise thee for I am fearfully and wonderfully made. Marvelous are thy works; And that my soul knoweth right well.

John 14-27 KJV Peace I leave with you; my peace I give to you. Not as the world gives do I give to you. Let not your hearts be troubled, neither let them be afraid.

There are people out there who do know how to render help and assistance. You must be willing to recognize it. One sitting or an appointment is not going to decide the decision or say one way or another if it is right or wrong. There may be several encounters, but they lead to the proper counsel and by the Holy Spirit designed to work specifically for you. Yes, you. No one said it is not ok to feel discouraged or tired. We all go through and bear something. Or even to feel embarrassed about. Everyone has something and if they deny it, they are lying not to you but to themselves. Whether it be an addiction, drugs or alcohol, sex, pornography, eating, whatever the case may be, there is something. We can carry something else called depression. Looking for a fix to cure it, which above with proper care and counseling continued, one can get it under control. I am not saying that one medicine traded for another will fix anything, but crying out on the inside is most definitely a cry out for help. God says I am your helper. The battle belongs to the Lord.

John 14-26 KJV But the Comforter, which is the Holy Ghost, whom the Father will send in my name, he shall teach you all things to your remembrance, whatsoever I have said unto you.

Romans 8-15 KJV For ye have not received the spirit of bondage again to fear, but ye have received the spirit of adoption, whereby we cry, Abba, Abba, Father.

Proverbs 16-9 KJV A man's heart deviseth his way; but the Lord directeth his steps.

I am writing this book in part to remembrance of the actor/musician Aron Carter. He was something special. He battled with a lot of demons and obstacles but always tried to show the bright side. Appearing to have a handle on things. A cheerful personality and a great persona. I was able to watch him and his mother Jane on a program called Marriage Bootcamp, a television series; and fell in love with them from the onset. You could see in his eyes his love for his mother and his willingness to overcome the obstacles in front of him. A true overcomer. His mother admitted to some things she had personally dealt with, and somewhat a placing of blame became a position of love and gratitude towards one another. He was reaching out to others, and you could see a great young man. Someone proud to call an achiever. Other things overcame him, and sadly, he passed this year. With his story and many more experiencing the same or similar, we can be who God has called us to be. Whether it be depression, events, addictions, being overworked, lack of funds, whatever the case may be, God is there for us.

1 Corinthians 10-13 KJV There hath temptation taken you but such as is common to man; but God is faithful, who will not suffer you to be tempted above that ye are able; but will with the temptation also make a way to escape, that ye may be able to bear it.

Matthew 11 28-30 KJV Come unto me, all ye that labour and are heavy laden, and

I will give you rest. Take my yoke upon you, and learn of me; for I am meek, and lowly in heart; and ye shall find rest unto your souls. For my yoke, it is easy, and my burden is light.

Proverbs 3 5-6 KJV Trust in the Lord with all thine heart; and lean not unto thine own understanding. In all thy ways acknowledge him, and he shall direct thy paths.

We can even be to one another a comfort under the guidance and expression of love that God has given to each one of us. Instead of being critical, judgmental, and self-absorbed. We are to show and distribute compassion and love to one another. Expecting nothing in return.

James 1 6-8 KJV But let him ask in faith, with no doubting, for he who doubts is like a wave of the sea driven and tossed by the wind. For let not that man suppose that he will receive anything from the Lord, he is a double-minded man, unstable in all his ways.

Chapter 2

When expectations and visions run high, are we basing it on ourselves and solely it is our way, or are we allowing God in to envision and wait to see what God has planned? Wait upon the Lord. It is in his timing and a journey for you to go through with and along with him.

Psalms 27-14 KJV Wait on the Lord; be of good courage, and he shall strengthen thine heart; wait I say, on the Lord.

Romans 8-28 KJV And we know that all things work together for good to them that love God, to them who are the called according to his purpose.

We can have goals that we are supposed to have, but when they become the very core of self, then we are disallowing God to work not only in us, but through us. He, God, has a master plan and is the creator of everything. Nothing is impossible with the Lord.

Luke 1-37 KJV For with God nothing is impossible.

This is when becoming overwhelmed and frustrated starts. You are thinking you can do it all, and it is not what God had planned for you. You are to be obedient unto God. He, God, did not design you to carry a load greater than you can carry.

Outlets and divisions start to creep in and set in, which adds to the aggravation. Thus putting you in a place you were not called to be in. Call upon him God, our creator. Derision such as a drink or drugs will not solve this issue or issues either. It will only compound them. Ultimately causing more blocks or internal agony. Seek, knock and ask, and you shall receive. God never breaks his promises. You are his son, his daughter. His child.

1 Peter 5-10 KJV But the God of all grace, who hath called us with a holy calling, not according to our works, but according to his own purpose and grace, which was given us in Christ Jesus before the world began.

Jeremiah 29-11 KJV For I know the thoughts that I think toward you, saith the Lord, thoughts of peace, and not of evil, to give you an expected end.

Habakkuk 2-3 KJV For the vision is yet for an appointed time, but at the end, it shall speak, and not lie; though it tarry, wait for it; because it will surely come, it will not tarry.

While reading this, I am hoping that you know Jesus as your savior and have accepted him as your savior.

If you have not, it does not matter how old, what gender, or anything that you can't stop and receive him as your personal savior.

You can invite and accept him as your personal savior: **Pray below**.

Please forgive me for my sins. I believe that you sent your Son Jesus to die on the cross for my sins.

I believe that you love me. I believe in my heart who you are. You are the Son of God. I confess with my mouth that I am a sinner. I accept you, Lord Jesus, as my savior. Please cleanse me from my sin and create a new and clean heart in me. I do believe that you are my savior and I now want to live for you as my Lord and my God. I know that I have eternal life in you because of the work you did on Calvary's Cross for me. Thank you, God. In Jesus name. Amen.

God is so wonderful and amazing.

The obstacles that one faces are a tremendous number of pressures and anxiety that one must deal with daily. Sometimes even being minute by minute. Our father never meant for any of his children to live a burdened, down, and broken life. People have expectations and truthfully, no one should live up to anyone's expectations. We are not designed or were we created in such a manner that we are robotic or made for someone else. We are made in the image of God. We have a destination and a purpose. We have gifts and talents bestowed on and upon us. We can try and play an instrument, say for example, and not be able to pick a string, read notes, or even remotely play with another, meaning it was not designed for you. Sure, you can try and master it, but if you were not designed to play it, you can pick and strum all day. I would say, pick something else up and try, and if not, well, there may be an opportunity in that field that you will excel at. Let God be your guide. It may be many gifts and talents you possess. Enjoy them all.

We can blame circumstances and make many excuses for not doing anything. However, if there is something in the way of progress and production, there are a few things in which you need to take a step and redirect the affirmations that have been spoken about your life and the destiny that you have in front of you. Each day, take a positive route toward what God has chosen for you to do. Yes, it is overwhelming. Faith is what you need to hold onto and imagine, as God is your anchor. He will complete what he has started and begun in you. Please believe this and hold onto it! When we do not see a way, God has a way. God knows the way, and he will make a way. Glory to our Father indeed. The anger or frustration is that of trying to do it all on your own and not relying on and, most of all believing that God is in charge. You may have tried and hit every block or jam and are angry. You have worked very hard and smacked one right after the other coming at you. Financially, you are hit in every direction and you see no way. You have a way. God is the way, the light, and most of all the creator of all. Stop trying to do it all in your own power. He, God, is the power and starts to realize that all is all and everything belongs to him. He will make a way. He already has a way designed. It is a journey that is joined with you and him. Enjoy this journey and all that encamps and unfolds around it. God is totally amazing. Even in difficulties, he will be right along with you. He will give you the strength to do and succeed.

Governing the soul inside is a lot of angst, which means that you are feeling compelled to do everything in your own way, by yourself, and no matter what the costs are involved. There is a big difference between dedication and control.

Same as honoring and glorifying God and being absorbed with one's own self. Sometimes, the darkness is the darkness that is created by the same. Self. We need to stand united and become compassionate about being there for one another. We need to reach out and connect with our Father and one another. Leading each one to the hands of the Father and standing in awe of how amazing he is, not ourselves. We can do anything by Christ, nothing is impossible. When you are weak, he is strong.

Hurting and Crying Out

You can start by restraining yourself or retraining yourself little by little. Something that is agitating and controlling you, you need to identify and recognize. Maybe not only make a mental note of it, but journal or write it down. Where you are aware of it, look at it and visually see where it is, that it bothers you, and where you might be able to make a difference by letting it bother you. Bringing it to and before our father. Praying for direction. Take steps to see a counselor who can lead you in the right direction. Sometimes, it may be an aversion to just wanting to hold onto you so tightly that you believe that everything rests on you. It does not rest on you. It is and belongs to God as everything in the universe does. God is our creator, and he created everything that exists. Step back and allow him to be your conductor and go with him in the direction in which he wants you to go. There is nothing as important as a deadline. If you can't make such and are putting the effort in, maybe it is them that need to step back a little bit. Allowing you to be who God created you to be, and to do what you know how to do, and to be the best at what you do. Contracts can always be renegotiated. Deadlines can be extended. God has a way and is the way. Sometimes, things are the bleakest before the doors swing open. Let the Lord propel you and move your steps and your thoughts. Nothing is so overwhelming that our father can't answer, does not have an answer and that you do not have an answer or outlet for. There are groups founded, check into them or on them. Each adversity has an answer. There is nothing so grand that it takes from you and steals your joy or purpose. To disrupt the visions that have come before you that you have worked on and dreamed about. If God gave you the vision, he, God, will certainly finish what he started. Do not ever give up or lose hope. All things work together for good, also in his timing.

There are organizations that assist in times of need or need. There are counselors in many fields. Doctors, friends. Dare to reach out and take the steps to get better and become who Christ has called you to be. Grace, Grace. He came so that we would have life more abundantly. Not broken down. He has where he has the power to give you a proper mindset if you will allow him the authority to come and live within you and your heart. No one ever said it would be an easy road, but it is an attainable one and a reachable one. God will never give you more than you can bear. He knows what you are capable of. If he has that assurance in you, assuredly rest in him and believe that you can do all things by Christ who strengthens you. He will never leave or forsake you.

If you are feeling pressured by calls demanding payments and threatening you to make them, and it is non-stop, do not allow this to threaten your existence in life and living life. You are a gift. God chose you, and no one has any right to ever make you feel that you are inadequate. You have options available to you. Payments, loans, family, and other routes. Before you claim bankruptcy, explore them. Do not let them take precedence over God and wait upon him. We will all go through something, and that something is bound to advance and perfect or prune you. Maybe for something better or for something you thought you were ready for and were not. Either way, there is nothing in the world or of the world worth allowing yourself the time to become depressed over or about and to end your life. Not anything or anyone. You can decide today, at this moment to make the change, and whatever little step it is, take it. I read a story about a young man, who had lost his wife and had two children. He was raising these two children who lost their mother. At some point, he sat and wrote a note about his feelings at that very moment. He needed ten thousand dollars to pay his bills but was having problems in trying to attain that amount. Feeling the pressure and loss, he decided to kill himself. This, he did, because of ten thousand dollars. The two children had no mother and now, no father. We have a father. He is there always to guide us. Call out to him, and where you may not see a way, there is a way.

There is always a way. God is divine. He will never ever leave you. Never let anything take hold of you without realizing that there is an answer. A positive and workable answer. When it seems like the entire world is falling apart, step away for a moment or two, disassociate yourself from the problem or the adversity and try to clear your head. Think about positive outcomes and possibilities that can alleviate the problem or problems. When you believe you can relate to them, then address them. God will give you the answers you are searching for. They may not be in the way in which you would like them, but he will provide for all your needs. Rest in him. Most of all be dependent upon God.

You can do this. There are active emergency centers you can call when you feel overwhelmed that will point you in the direction you need to go. Never think it is not worth it. You are totally worth it.

Chapter 3

If you are in a relationship and you believe you are in one that is your soul mate, that is wonderful. Always add to it and bring the special quality that started and attracted you to them in the first place flowing. Our father is in the relationship too. Ask and you shall receive. However, if you are in a relationship that is demanding and controlling stop to ask yourself if this is a relationship or a dominion that allows the other to distort what true love is. It is not mind-altering, controlling, or abusive. It is not demanding one's own way and threatening in any sort of way. It is Godly and as of God. Loving, kind, compassionate, and most of all pure. Do not settle for anything that compromises who God created you to be. Making a choice between them or others, family, God, children, etc. God is about love, and we abound in love when we are walking in the perfect love of Christ. Nor is it a choice to check out if the person leaves, abandons, or threatens you in a way that brings them control over you. That is not love and you can't fix them or their problems or issues. You can be there for them and supportive. However, do not sell yourself short by trying to make it into something that it is not or never will be. God is the way, the truth and the life. Believe in God and the directions in which he places you in are totally where God has you and your destiny set to be. Inside we hear or are saying, you don't know. We love each other, it is different or not as you think. Excuses for behavior or plain rejection/cover up.

God speaks. God can use others as mouthpieces. But we must be willing to listen and to also submit to the word of God. He is saying,

I am near. I will never leave or forsake you. A strong confident foundation. Sometimes it takes drastic actions and in others, it is a process.

No one has a right in love or any other reason to beat you. To lay hands on you of any kind. You are and were wonderfully made by the hand of God. His love is a perfect and formed love. Pure and noble. Whether the abuse is physical or verbal, it is abuse and abusive. By the authority of God's word, let the weak say I am strong. You will weather this storm and be ok. God supplies our needs daily. You were not created to be broken. You are a daughter/son in Christ.

A relationship is like getting on a boat and setting sail. It has many adventures and adversities it will encounter. It is not and never will be on course, full steam ahead. To say so, would be fooling yourself. Inside we hear or are saying, you don't know. He is different. She is different. We love each other, it is different. Excuses for behavior plain rejection/cover up. There are no excuses. God speaks. God can also use others as a mouthpiece. There are also signs one should be aware of those details, exactly the course and behavior of the individual. But we must be willing to listen to the word of God. He is saying, I am near. I will never leave you or forsake you. A strong, confident foundation. Sometimes, it takes drastic actions and in others, it is a process.

No one has a right in love or any other reason to beat you, to lay hands on you of any kind. Hurting people hurt others. Do not fall into that place. Let God, direct your steps.

It takes two to guide and nourish. Adding and growing daily. Seeing and hearing one another. More importantly, hearing and listening to one another. Being there for one another. Daily adding love and showing love to one another. Knowing and making known that they are important. God says, we are to love unconditionally all. Never take one for granted. Never use them for gain or putting your expectations upon them, limiting them from who God called them to be. Working together to achieve the goals you set. You both, not singularly. Knowing that you are not alone. God is with you always. In the course, you may encounter some difficulties. Lack of funds, death, a move from comfortable surroundings, a job promotion or closure, health, whatever it may be, be joyful in all things, in all circumstances. Holding onto and building one another up. God will sustain you and lead you through and to where the place and his destiny are for you. Holding onto and building one another up. Seeking God's ways, God promises and always depend on God wholeheartedly. It is not the circumstances that make things bad, it is how you respond to those circumstances that expel actions.

Feelings. Feelings come and go. If we acted on our feelings and emotions, which I think the average person has about 35,000 feelings daily, we would all be basket cases. We are to think of pure, lovely, true, and noble things. When doubt, disbelief, alarm, or worry creep up- STOP- swipe them to the left, and then replace it with a positive thought. It is not easy, but God says, my yoke is easy. My yoke is light.

Every relationship that is lasting takes work and time. With God connected and not just in the vows spoken in a wedding ceremony but for always and throughout, you can do all things through Christ, who strengthens you. Nothing is to difficult for God or impossible. Remember, it is in his timing, not yours. Nothing ever comes without work. To incorporate God into the marriage is what brings happiness through and through, as God says he will never leave you. Count on that!

John 14-6 NIV Jesus answered, "I am the way the truth and the life. No one comes to the Father except through me."

Matthew 6-33 KJV But seek ye first the Kingdom of God, and his righteousness; and all these things shall be added unto you.

Galatians 2-20 KJV I am crucified with Christ, nevertheless I live; yet not I, But Christ liveth in me; and the life which I now live in the flesh I live by the faith of the Son of God, who loved me, and gave himself for me.

1 Corinthians 13-1 NIV Love is patient, love is kind. It does not envy, it does not boast, it is not proud. It is not rude, it is not self-seeking, it is not easily angered, it keeps no record of wrongs. Love does not delight in evil but rejoices with the truth.

Hebrews 13 5-6 KJV Let your conversation be without covetousness; and be content with such things as ye have; for he hath said; I will never leave thee. So that we may boldly say, The Lord is my helper, and I will not fear what man shall do unto me.

Proverbs 16-9 KJV "A man's heart deviseth his way; but the Lord directeth his steps."

Proverbs 3 5-6 KJV Trust in the Lord with all thine heart; and lean not unto thine own understanding.

In all thy ways acknowledge him, and he shall direct thy paths.

Psalm 34 18-19 NIV The Lord is near to the brokenhearted and saves the crushed in spirit.

Many are the afflictions of the righteous, but the Lord delivers him out of them all.

Chapter 4

Loneliness is a huge issue for many. You can be in a room full of people and even a spouse/mate and feel alone. So, it is not singled out to, loneliness. There are a lot of issues that trigger these feelings, and it is best to understand why you are feeling this way. You may even want to seek help or medical attention, as it could be a culprit of depression, which some suffer from, which may need medicine to treat short-term or long-term. Others are going through some things and or dump their issues on you, which is another issue, and the death of a loved one is another too. Underlying undiagnosed symptoms may also be within, but each one needs to be dealt with and not acted on. There are many reasons to experience a chilly feeling or feelings. Again, do not act on them, seek assistance for treatment.

Hurting and Crying Out

God says he will guide the path in which you take and walk along with you on it. We are all unique and wonderfully made. Not everyone is the same, so the tolerance that you have and another, are completely different. You may meet someone and share what it is you are encountering, and they may be able to share some of the things you are going through and that they went through. Lifting one another up. However, do not force what you went through or expect them to experience the same outcome as you. Again, each is an individual. Accept them as that, and do not put any expectations on them. Do not criticize or judge them either. He, God is our light and salvation. A glorious wonder. No weapon formed against you will prosper. Be strong and of good courage. Within you is the light shining through, and you can connect, see yourself as more than a conqueror. You can overcome any obstacle that is in your path or trying to block you. Nothing is impossible for our father. Not anything. Everything takes time and effort. Be willing to make that change and surrender everything into his hands. Jesus declared, it is finished, and it was. By his blood, if you have accepted him personally as your savior, he died for your sins, and you are the righteousness of God through Christ, where it has been added to your account, and God holds you blameless. Putting on the whole armor of God. You can overcome.

Sometimes, allowance is wallowing in self-pity and denial. If this seems to be something that you are doing again, put on the whole armor of God and start to move towards the place God has designed you to go. You take and follow what God has chosen for you to do. Stand strong and be victorious. Not only stand strong, but say aloud you are victorious. You will see changes on the horizon if you try and make an effort. Everything is a process. We are all someone from somewhere, and we need to remember we are loved. Truly loved.

If someone is dumping all their troubles on you unduly, do not accept them. You can only do so much. With God, nothing is impossible.

An excerpt from Richard Foster, writes, Loneliness is inner emptiness. Solitude is inner fulfillment. Solitude is a state of mind and heart.

We may be screaming out for contact, but sometimes separation is key to fundamentally becoming all that God has in store for you. Quietly waiting for what he, God, has designed for you and has in store for you. The responses you take or exude are key elements of success and overcoming. Jesus did not come for you to have life and to live difficult. He came so that you would have life more abundantly. Receive the word and incorporate it into your life and daily activities, and you will see the manifestation of how amazing God is. It is not assured that you will not face trials or even various at the same time, but keeping and affirming. The right attitude will make the events less frustrating and prevent them from wearing you down. When you take control, you are not allowing God to do anything. When you become overly into numerous undertakings and then push to where it becomes explosive or to the point of hurting another, you have taken on too much. Doing what you are not called to handle and do, and most of all, not allowing God to do. With anything it is a team. Father, Son, and Holy Spirit. A terrific team indeed. Disassociate yourself and take a deep breath, pray, and then go back to. If you meet the same obstacles, you might want to take a night to pray and a new approach to it in the morning. Dare to watch what God can do.

Sometimes, we watch while our friends suddenly disappear, and we have done nothing to create or cause adversity. This can be trying if you have ever experienced it. Instead of trying to figure it out and becoming discouraged and sad, remain positive and be there for them. Sometimes, it is God moving people out so he can create a new chapter in your life. So, where you may be heading or going to begin, they are not in the big picture. It is not up to us to figure things out. We are to lean on God. Open our hearts and minds to what God has in store for us. An old saying is Change does not make an appointment with any of us, it just shows up. So true. Some like to be in total control of their future and seeing how we do not know what it is, we can't do this. Nor predict the future or the outcome. Hope is putting everything into what Christ has called us each to do. One thing for sure is you are never alone.

Nothing is done at a moment's notice or nanosecond. Everything takes time. However, it requires an effort from you, and if you take the steps and the alternatives to properly execute a better today, then tomorrow will begin to be a little bit easier and with God, all things ARE possible!!

God's promises are never broken. God will take your broken pieces and put them together as he has ordained from the onset of your creation and what you are destined to do and be. You are a champion, dare to believe that. Victory is yours, believe that.

There are new beginnings, new people, new avenues, and new places. Let God do what God does best: love you. In the process, love yourself too. The journey with God is incredible. I call it my team. Father, Son, and Holy Spirit. One can never go wrong with God.

Proverbs 16-9 ESV The heart of man plans his way, but the Lord establishes his steps.

Psalm 139- 14 NIV I praise you because I am fearfully and wonderfully made; your works are wonderful; I know that full well.

Romans 10-9 KJV "That if thou shalt confess with thy mouth the Lord Jesus, and shalt believe in thine heart that God hath raised him from the dead, thou shalt be saved."

1 Peter 2-9 NIV But you are a chosen people, a royal priesthood, a holy nation. God's special possession, that you may declare the praises of him who called you out of darkness into his wonderful light.

John 15 −16 ESV You did not choose me, but I chose you and appointed you so that you might go and bear fruit- fruit that will last- and so that whatever you ask in my name the Father will give you.

Lamentations 3-26 KJV It is good that a man should both hope and quietly wait for the salvation of the Lord.

Isaiah 40-31 KJV But they that wait upon the Lord shall renew their strength; they shall mount up with wings as eagles; they shall run, and not be weary; and they shall walk, and not faint.

Joshua 1-8 NIV Keep this Book of the Law always on your lips; meditate on it day and night, so that you may be careful to do everything written in it. Then you will be prosperous and successful.

Psalm 119-15 NIV I meditate on your precepts and consider your ways.

Romans 3 3-5 KJV And not only so, but we glory in tribulations also; knowing that tribulation worketh patience;

And patience, experience; and experience, hope;

And hope maketh not ashamed; because the love God is shed abroad in our hearts by the Holy Ghost which is given unto us.

Chapter 5

Things are coming at full speed ahead, and you are wondering how in the world you are going to handle them. The operative word here is how you are going to handle it. We can do nothing apart from God. You have overtaken and gone beyond what the human mind can imagine, and the workload is extreme. Where did this arise or come about? Was it a vision or a dream? Did you receive word that you were all there is and only you can do all the things as no one else knows how to do anything? Delegation of duties and teamwork makes a dream happen. Without proper authority, things can become chaotic. The key here is before it becomes a dream or a vision, God the Father placed it in your heart. God is the one who is the author and the finisher. You do nothing alone. Acknowledge God. Acknowledge that you do have weaknesses.

Hurting and Crying Out

Once you access this, stop and look at what it is that you want to achieve. Design, the thought process, going to the drawing board. Many minds have a place and patterns are drawn by connections. As well as success. What you have visualized, put down and start the walk. The walk with Christ. Making mental notes is good, but start writing them down. God has already designed them.

This preparation will leave you not drained, overwhelmed, and at peace.

You relinquish this and surrendering it to God will fill you with energy, joy, and the ability to give totally to the project or projection of what you would like to accomplish and help you to set out to do.

If you are done pushing yourself, believing that you are the only one and making it so, you cut off more than you can imagine and you set yourself up for the letdown.

Timing is in God's hands. The entirety of the dream, event, vision, calling, requires God. Serving yourself almost always represents strain, stress, or even failure.

Reservation is preservation. You can overcome any challenge that is presented in God's timing, not yours. Relatively speaking it is and all does truly belong to God.

You will be in zinc when you walk with the Father, and the journey is with God.

There is so much joy in his application. To also say, that is a wonderful delight.

If you dare to imagine, you can see that it will be a vision of beauty indeed.

God says that he knows the plans he has for you! Plans to prosper and of hope.

If God knows his plans, which are his plans, where is it written that you control and are in control? Frustration is not in the word of God or his promises. Nor does God say, do it your way. God is the way.

You can see a dream come to fruition and give yourself to the music and the melody. Creating it, along with God, is the best concert on point. The journey along with God in it will avail much. Taking each step with him, God, you can see your dream, dreams, and vision give birth and succeed.

Effort/efforts do not come without stress, delays, or mishaps. With God and your responses to and actions avail much. We are to find joy in all things.

God says, be strong and of good courage. Keep a joyful attitude. Ven when something arises, as it will eventually. Some things go smoothly, and others have a train of ups and downs.

When you are in a calming state and along with God in things distressing, they will turn into an answer or a resolution. It will work to the success of the structure you are trying to attain, not destroy.

If they become so overwhelming, step away for a moment and try to regroup and if, even that means a day away from. There is nothing worse than fighting and struggling with yourself. That will give you time to go into prayer and pray about including the ability to access what could be a simple solution or a complicated one. Even to seek advisement over.

We are to serve God and work as if we are working for God. Not man or unto man. Always doing your best and being your best.

Wait upon God and rest in God.

Keep your heart open, your mind fixed on God, and your goals. Praying and being thankful for all things. Encouraging and lifting one another. Not strife.

Youth or called the next generation, stop and listen to them as technology changes rapidly daily. Wisdom appears from many places, known and unknown. Be open and receptive to ideas. God can use many and much to enlighten us.

Never think you know everything. God created the world and everything in it. You do **not** do anything alone or solely by yourself. It is

God's and by God. His grace and his mercy. Humble yourselves before him. Each step is a process.

It is and is known to be in God's timing. Submit yourself to God's timing and his plans for you. You will watch them unfold and feel at ease. Being in God's steps for you and along with you.

Do not give up, quit, or lose hope.

Work towards your dreams and goals. Waiting upon the Lord. Keep being active in what God has called you to do and other projects. Not allowing the enemy to enter to steal, rob, or kill your joy. Be content in all things, even in and speaking of adversities. Stand strong in God's promises. These things that overwhelm you and against you shall pass. Do not give life to them. Remain in God's hands and guidance.

If you have accepted Jesus as your savior, it is by his blood you can claim all his promises. Jesus died for our sins, yours and mine. We are the righteousness of God, which Jesus credited to our account, and God sees us as blameless.

Therefore, you may claim what God has promised. One of Six the Armor of God's. Hold steadfast to what God promises and never let go or forget the King of Kings.

Some things you may want, God may want you to have more or thrust you beyond what your dreams are. Pray and speak to him about all things. Never wavering. Trust in God, not yourself.

Do not claim the enemy's or any attacks. Do not let negativity drive you.

If you open that window or door, the air of negativity will blow in all kinds of memories, baggage packed from memory lane, and on anything else you, yes you allow to dwell, think on, or even blame. When this starts, stop yourself, take a breath, and swipe it to the left. Do not let the frustration build; it grows to it's an explosion state. Recognize it and go to God. Get up, do something else (to change the thought patterns), take a walk, re-focus, and again, pray. Pray our

Father guides you and gives you a hedge of protection that surrounds you and encompasses you with his love. To reset your mind with good thoughts.

It may even take a day or two, but it may be that when all is said and done, it will all go smoothly and as it should. Seeking God and his ways.

All things take work.

There is nothing difficult for God or impossible. When you do not have the answers, seek them in the proper forms. Be it research, hiring teams, consultation, counselors, therapy. Sources are out there and are available.

There is nothing to quit, lose hope or destroy yourself over. You can become your own worst enemy and nightmare. When you see this as an expression of your feelings, which a lot of people use, deflect from that. Stop having a pity party and embrace yourself with love and the love for God. In all things with thanksgiving, let your supplications be known and made to God. Praying about everything, resting totally and hoping in God.

Can start with this: I have been crucified with Christ; it is no longer. I who live, but Christ lives in me, and the life which I now live in the flesh I live by faith in the Son of God, who loved me and gave himself for me. Galatians 2:20.

Jeremiah 29-11 NIV For I know the plans I have for you, declares the Lord, plans to prosper you and not to harm you, plans to give you hope and a future.

Joshua 1-9 KJV Have not I commanded thee? Be strong and of good courage; be

not afraid neither be thou dismayed, for the Lord thy God is with thee withersoever thou goest.

Philippians 4-7 NIV And the peace of God, which transcends all understanding will guard your hearts and your minds in Christ Jesus.

1 PETER 5 6-7 ESV Humble yourselves, therefore under the mighty hand of God so that at the proper time he may exalt you.

Casting all your anxieties on him, because he cares for you.

Chapter 6

God says my peace, which passes all understanding.

That is a verse within itself. Ponder it. Think about it and what it means.

His (God's) ways are higher than our ways. What does that mean to you? That you know best? That you can incorporate some of your own with his and join them together and it is the best? No, it means his ways are. His ways are higher than yours, mine, and ours. God created the entire universe; do you honestly think anything is too difficult for him?

His thoughts (not yours) are higher than ours. (You do not know everything).

The enemy wedges (comes against) us in our thoughts, our actions, and in our weaknesses.

What we do not understand, God does.

We do not always get an instant answer. God is on the spot and along with us. God knows, hears, and sees all.

No, it does not make sense at what is happening or forming. No, it is not easy. No, it does not have an instant repair patch or easy access to not feel.

What? Feel?

Yes, you are feeling the enemy's attack.

It may feel like a light swat to a full-blown self-pity party or an attack all out. Be strong and of good courage.

Do not play into this. God makes a way and an escape.

God is the way.

When Satan sees something promoting the kingdom of God and your love, he casts out warfare and we fight daily. Put on the entire Armor of God.

God provides comfort, strength, protection, and safety in his mighty wings. He will cover and shield you.

Rest, rest in him, God.

Today in our world there is so much angst, bitterness, and people hurting one another. They believe they are entitled. To this point of hurting one another.

They may even try to go on a crusade of murder and mayhem to prove their point or points which they believe they have. Again, the enemy's attack.

To arrive at this point, it must be festering and no one is paying any heed to it or concern. It usually is after and then the need to review, when in all reality the person is and has been crying out all along. We need not only to show more compassion to one another, but we actually need to pay more attention to one another and what they are saying. Listening is a key not, yeah, I hear you. That is a vague response indeed. Point them in the right direction, get involved as love comes freely to all of us and it costs nothing. Care about one another. God says we are to love all unconditionally.

If you see something unusual, try to reach out and help them. Get help or tell someone your concerns. Not saying anything is not helping them. It could prevent rage that results later. Into schools, a store, or other events to killing sprees.

We are the family of God. God goes to look for and after his lost sheep. We are his sheep. Yes, even the one from the one hundred.

Hurting and Crying Out

God cares and loves us all unconditionally. Love has no conditions, nor is I will have and do things my way or ways attached to it. It is love, divine and true love. Being obedient unto God.

Not only try to encourage them, encourage yourself.

Sometimes, there are reasons behind actions, but more than often not the way we respond and act are more crucial than the events or circumstances themselves.

To replace inactive, nonproductive, ungodly, unkind, and unknown thoughts, and feelings, do it with godly thoughts. God's thoughts. Verses applied, repeat them, and let your heart receive them. Upload them in the corner of your mind and you will see God prevail. Everything starts with something small. God is big and never-ending and will always be there.

Endure and you will see God's love measured.

The battle belongs to the Lord. Surrender fully into his hands. Let him direct your steps and path. Do not try to pick it up in your own will and stance.

You are never alone. He is with you in all things. Sometimes, you may not know, but he was the one carrying you when you were most lost or broken. Our father is amazing, yes, amazing.

People hurt one another and yes, it does hurt.

Whether it is hurting people, hurting others because they hurt, or our friends, who by no exception hurt us by jealousy, fear, or not being a friend (true) false, it hammers down into our very core to someone making a false allegation, accusation, or to even a no like comment on your media profile. No matter what it is, go to God. Ask our Father to give you strength. We can't control others, but we have control by God of our thoughts and have the right mindset. Your response, your connection to the circumstance, connect, or disconnect is vital. Not retaliation.

There is not any point in proving a point as it holds no value except to antagonize the other person or event.

You can show or speak about it later. Two or more angry people do not hear one another.

Decide to choose your issues and let Father, Son, and Holy Spirit direct your steps and your path.

The Bible, God's word, is the best counselor, directorate, love map, light, and foundation to name a phenomenal list you and I have at our hands. So put it in your hands, and use it for its purpose, as a gift of love and compass to the amazing discovery of true love.

True compassion, living life, living in victory, real promises. Start today if you haven't already and see that God is amazing. Amazing. Seek him.

Little by little, you will see God reveal the truth and his words will come bursting out as you set yourself free from incriminations.

Nothing is too difficult for God.

Some things might not seem fair, or no answers, or there is so much happening at the same time. You may not understand why, and it boggles you to the point of obsession. Your response is boiling, and you are totally upset. Stand strong and take a step away from the situation and disassociate yourself from it. Nothing is that important to ever steal your joy or your peace. God gives us grace and it is sufficient for all things. He, God, never gives us anything that we can't bear.

Isaiah 55 8-9 KJV For my thoughts are not your thoughts, neither are your ways my ways, saith the Lord.

For as the heavens are higher than the earth, so are my ways higher than your ways, and my thoughts than your thoughts.

Psalm 32 7 NIV You are my hiding place; you will protect me from trouble and surround me with songs of deliverance.

Romans 12-2 KJV And be not conformed to this world; but be transformed by the renewing of your mind, that ye may prove what is good, and acceptance and perfect will of God.

Deuteronomy 31-8 NLT Do not be afraid or discouraged for the Lord will personally go ahead of you. He will be with you; he will neither fail you nor abandon you.

Jeremiah 32-27 KJV "Behold, I am the Lord, the God of all flesh; is there anything to hard for me?"

Titus 2 11-14 NIV For the grace of God has appeared that offers salvation to all people. It teaches us to say "NO" to ungodliness and worldly passions, and to live self-controlled upright and godly lives in this present age, while we wait for the blessed hope- the appearing of the glory of our great God and Savior, Jesus Christ who gave himself for us to redeem us from all wickedness and to purify for himself people that are his very own, eager to do what is good.

Chapter 7

You are the righteousness of God in Christ.

Christ suffered much.

Persecution, rejection, unbelief, abandonment, stoning, many things. He, Jesus, hung on the cross and died on the cross for your and my sins.

As he, Jesus is our savior and by his blood, we are forgiven. We are forgiven for our sins.

There is no lack of his bloodshed, poverty, sickness, love, it is bound by his blood shed on the cross for you and me.

We will prosper. We will have no more lack, as it is written. We will have health; we will prosper and not be in lack. Words have life, and we are to speak life into them. He came so that we could have life more abundantly.

It is the enemy who stacks thoughts of disillusions and uses weaknesses of each against. Trying to convince you of God, not fulfilling his promises. All lies, do not believe the enemy. Such as divorce, poverty, loss, illness, death, and so on. When it is always God that is there alongside of you always. With you and loving you unconditionally. Be ye strong in the Lord.

Casting all your concerns unto and with him. God.

God is not only with you and along with you, but he does also know what is best.

We see what we want.

God sees what is best and what is good.

If you have, and you have not thanked God for all you have, and you are wanting more, and you are complaining about what you have, you continue on a spiral of insult and agony. Why would you get more or larger? It would be more complaints. To have more would mean more work, more effort, more costs, and you would become overwhelmed. If you can't contend and maintain with what you do have and be grateful for, larger would not be what you would need until you grasp what you do have and what you do with it. God is kind and certainly would not want you overwhelmed. Making excuses as to if you did have, you would do this or that, is not an answer either. It is what you do with what you have and how you handle that things progress and multiply. Praise God because he does know what is best. Therefore, in all things, with thanksgiving let your requests be known. Praying to God. Your prayers and your visions may not be as directly as you see, but they could be even more, as God has designed all.

God, as the creator, has designed a masterpiece. Each of us has talents and beautiful gifts.

God also does not give us what we can't handle either. So, where or what it is that you do, seek, or want may be crafted into excellence at where you are.

Think wisely and work diligently. Remembering how truly amazing our father is.

Dare to dream big and always remember who your (our) creator is. Nothing is impossible. It is Christ who strengthens us. The enemy

(Satan) is full of lies. Nothing, no weapon formed against us shall prosper. Repeat it because God never breaks his promises. His love is pure, unconditional, and forever. He has only the best in his heart for you and me. There is no right to feel as if you are owed something. As it all belongs to the Lord. It is the Lord that blesses us and supplies all our needs. In some instances, we may lose something, but what we gain through the process is more than what we lose. It can be a very precious crossing. We will go through and suffer things. Some more than others and maybe not even others. Be strong and of good courage.

Naturally, it will not come easy to some. God knows us inside and out. Don't ever quit or give up on yourself. He knows our future, and the future is in his hands.

Our dreams, our hopes, desires. Every fiber thought or action, God knows. He knows our shortness, our weaknesses, lusts. If we try and each day takes a step towards our calling, we can. You can achieve much and work towards what you were called, born to do, and be. Let God direct your steps.

Honor and glorify God. Praise and thanksgiving.

The best team to have is the Father, the Son, and the Holy Spirit.

Can't do wrong with the best crew ever. Seek ye, the kingdom and all will be added.

That says a lot. How inspiring, how creative, how wonderful and marvelous God is.

Don't be wondering about your tomorrow when God has blessed you with today.

Take his hand as he goes before you and is with you. Enjoy the day you have, and along with God in it. The beauty he is. God has created it and is totally beauty.

The journey goes hand in hand, and it can be an exciting journey if you surrender it unto him as your savior and know him as your savior. Watch what and how amazing he is.

Without him, you can do nothing. With him, all things are possible. Keep this thought in mind. Instill it into the depths of your heart.

You can become so rigid with working and increase that you forget in an instant you can lose it all. You did not do anything by yourself. God has been standing along with you and as he is now. He knew the beginning and the end before it ever evolved. It is magnificent to depend on God and work side by side with him. If ever a true love was known, it is the genuine true love for our father. His love for us is unquestionable without doubt but always constant never wavering.

Step back and take account of all that is transpiring and go to prayer if confused. Father, Son, and Holy Spirit will direct your steps totally.

It is a privilege to be able to worship and love God. Always bring glory to him.

You can wait patiently while in his timing, and by his will, he will bring his promises (which should be yours too) to pass and to fruition.

Stand strong in all things. Do not magnify your problems magnify your father.

Start today.

Work and release, lift all your concerns to God.

Yes, you need an answer.

God is the answer.

God knows and sees our concerns, hurts, and confusion. God gives us a sound mind. We are to think about what is noble, true, pure, and lovely. These thoughts placed in lieu of other non-constructive thoughts lead to a better way of life and living life.

Change of patterns and waiting on the Lord is the best. You can be reassured that God hears you.

You can't control anything, but you can respond properly. You can wait to see the goodness of God. Most importantly, surrender yourself and your thoughts to him.

If he can feed 5000, with five loaves and two fish, how much more can he do for you or me?

The magnitude in which God moves is astonishing. Fear produces nothing! Fear is a culprit of Satan.

We all experience it. Experience it and even embrace it and then let it go, kick it aside, and move forward with God and in God's perfect peace. Do not ever let it rule you.

That is what you want to experience: God's perfect love and peace, which passes all understanding. Affirm it and receive it today.

Sometimes, people don't need perfection, they relate to flaws. God loves us all our flaws included. However, if we were made in the image of God, we do not have any flaws. God is perfectly and wonderfully made. See yourself as that.

2 Corinthians 5-21 KJV For he hath made him to be sin for us, who knew no sin; that we might be made righteousness of God in him.

John 15-5 NIV "I am the vine; you are the branches. If you remain in me and I in you, you will bear much fruit; apart from me you can do nothing.

Isaiah 26-3 KJV Thou will keep him in perfect peace, whose mind is stayed on thee; because he trusteth in thee.

Chapter 8

Strengths and weaknesses. Each in various stages, different among and in each of us.

God says, be strong and of good courage.

Let the weak proclaim, I am strong.

Make the blind to see and the deaf to hear.

Our father is not only pretty amazing, but he is also just as it is written.

God the father (our father) also does not give us anything for which we can't bear or escape from. In all things be content. Situations are subject to change. If you put a key in a lock, it will not open. Nothing you face is permanent or etched in stone. Even in death you move forward or backward. So maybe, yourself, you choose to be frozen in the events. However, the day is and will be just as the sun comes up and sets. God is with you.

Take a moment to reflect, acknowledge, praise, and being thankful. God will speak, lead, open make a way if you will open your heart and your ears to him.

Strength is already within, tap into it, as the source is God. Not only you have God the Father, Christ the Son, and the Holy Spirit. You can, we can do all things through Christ, who strengthens us.

Nothing is impossible with God.

That says it.

Proclaim it. Receive it. Believe it.

You, my dear, will achieve it.

We can choose to demand our own way, or we can surrender ourselves to God and wait patiently for him to work, to answer, and to do all he has created us to do and be. Keep on striving to work unto God and loving him so much that you know his plans, his ways, and his will are nothing but the best. Have a personal relationship and fellowship with him.

The NOW factor could be, but the YOU factor generally.

You want, you did, you think, you demand, you gave. Maybe so, but where is God in this? Where is his will and who is he considered? Is it your will be done? No! It is shallow-based thinking.

Have you thought beyond your expectations? Costs, safety, are you ready, complaints, strength, team, a lot goes into everything. From great to small.

Details and he (God) our father is the master of alignment. He knows his plans for you and in all things. You do not predict the future or others in it. He knows the channels. He is the channel. The way, the truth, and the light. Walk this way.

Happiness is walking in and experiencing God in all that you do or undertake.

True joy and exhilaration.

Is your heart full of love for the father?

Strength within exhumes out of love that fills the heart of God. The smile that comes across your face is the joy of our Lord, loving God as no one or nothing else. That is joy and strength.

Joel 3-10 KJV Beat your plow shares into swords and your pruning hooks into spears; let the weak say I am strong.

1 Corinthians 10-13 KJV "There hath no temptation taken you, but such as is common to man; but God is faithful, who will not suffer you to be tempted above that ye are able; but will with the temptations also make a way to escape, that ye may be able to bear it."

Proverbs 3 5-6 NIV Trust in the Lord with all your heart and lean not on your own understanding; in all your ways submit to him, and he will make your paths straight.

Chapter 9

There are many forms of crying out.

Many picturesque faces.

Those of true hurt.

Those of real life, years of pain and hurt.

Every one of them is false. It is the enemy's attack coming in and allowing it to overcome and overwhelm us.

We are made in the image of God. God is our comforter and our provider in everything. In all things.

It is real: the pain, the suffering, and the angst. However, how we receive it and respond to it is what makes the difference in not letting it overtake us.

Yes, you are hurting.

Yes, you are in pain, but God says to take hold of his yoke. Take hold of him in all things.

Jesus died the ultimate death, and by his blood, it is finished. No more pain, no longer lack or inability.

Say it. It is finished. By his blood, Jesus, I will prosper nothing, <u>no</u> weapon formed against me will prosper. I will have and live life more abundantly. I shall be well and whole. No sickness shall have me. I am not, nor will I accept the poison the enemy wants and forms against me. Not now or ever. I am whole and wonderfully made in the image of Christ.

I am forgiven for my sins, and I accept that. I believe it too.

Come to him that is weary (worn out), and he, God, will give you rest.

It is a battlefield out there every day. Prepare yourself and not become or associate with the toxic or toxins. Jesus changed water into wine. Something beautiful happens when you allow Jesus to be your savior and change you. You allow God to move totally in your life and the Holy Spirit for direction and intercession, you have something wonderful called, Peace!

A peace which passes all understanding.

Divine!

Hurting and Crying Out

Don't let the years allow you to shed those tears.

Embrace them, acknowledge them, but more importantly, open up your heart to God. Give those tears, hurts, pains, and difficulties to him.

When you cry out for Jesus, our Father, your heart is open and full.

Full of love, full of compassion, and those my sons and daughters are tears you shall want to cry out for. Yahweh. Abba. Our heavenly father.

His presence.

An everlasting, eternal presence.

Let the things of the past move to where they belong.

In the past!

Embrace yourself too! You are on this journey. You are not alone.

You may physically be alone, but you are never alone. God is omnipresent. Never leaving or forsaking you. You are strong in the Lord. More than a conqueror.

You can do all things through Christ who strengthens you. Nothing is impossible with God and in God Always focus on our heavenly father.

Renewing of the mind. Putting on a new mindset. It is daily and we need to do this. Little by little, you CAN, and you will achieve the happiness and life God has designed for you.

Don't waste it.

As I said before, life is a journey and a beautiful journey that God has designed specifically for you and me.

Do not hold onto but, and but, you don't know what I have been through, he or she really hurt me, they left me, I do <u>not</u> have, I can't.

Honey, you can! Yes, you **CAN**!!! Say it until you know it and do it.

God created you in his image, not your image. Dare to imagine what you CAN DO because of Christ. Manifest your heart on that. With God all things are possible.

They did this and that. Some truths, excuses. Some just denial- Reach in and pull that tab from so what? Are you going to blame them all your life? Are you going to stop growing and being all you were created to be because of them or the circumstances?

Lord, I want to be all you created me to be and more.

To honor and serve you. To bring you glory dear Lord.

Then, have the journey- don't buy that ticket and stay on the train of circles, never arriving but departing over and over again. Try yes, but do not repeat the same mistakes over. Every effort is seen by God, so God knows and will lead you on the right path.

Cast your cares upon him-God.

He cares for you.

I am weak, I can't.

Let the weak say, I am strong.

Each day is a gift and a new day -start there!

Being thankful. Call it (new beginnings).

Put off, no, pull off, that OLD and put on the NEW.

God is so awesome and amazing.

Wasting is sad and it saddens the soul, and it robs it. A life of joy, peace, and happiness it could have known.

The enemy is always happy sand working to prevent you from living for God.

With God and what God has ordained in your life.

See through the mask. Every day he prowls to rob, kill, and destroy.

No longer do we have to live like that.

Hurting and Crying Out

God is the answer and the way.

You are as talented and gifted as anyone else and we all have gifts and talents.

We should always admire one and their talents and enjoy.

We may learn we may have that gift or want it (and not), we may teach it reach out it has many facets, but gratitude?

Gratitude is it!! Be thankful to God in all things. Ye of little faith. Believe.

Faith as small as a mustard seed can produce so, you can, you can achieve.

Reach out to God and wait upon him. God will never ignore or abandon us.

You can't demand your own way or is it in your own timing. Be patient and wait upon the Lord. It may ignite and take off right away, or it may take months or years. God has his way, and he knows what he is doing. Be patient.

Everything has its purpose and there is a season for the purpose. In season and in God's will, you will reap. The manifestation is God's. Let God, be God.

One day soon, or in the future, you will stand, shining and smiling at what God has called you to do and be. Find joy in all things.

In writing, I often feel his presence and the joy in my heart, so I know that in all things, God is JOY! God is with us.

You might even say it's too hard, you don't have the education, money, people, but God says you can do all things through him.

Not by power, not by might, but by my spirit, you will succeed.

Stop the tears. Put the Kleenex away.

Accept Jesus as your personal savior. Start building on his promises. Not lies or letdowns.

Don't let days turn into years.

Each day, you start and he will walk with you.

Magnify your God and he will magnify your future.

Transformation begins with you. Today, declare it over your life.

You are loved.

You too, now love yourself. He, God, will guide you. Always!

What you have been through and are going through, God has walked in with you and through. He pulled you through and still remains walking with you in. So, let all that go now- thank him for everything, and progress forward for the CALL he, God has called you for. You will be amazed at all he does, can do, and will do. Most importantly, it has already been done. Gratitude and Praise go hand in hand. Stop now to praise him, to thank him.

Genesis 1-27 NIV So God created mankind in his own image, in the image of God he created them; male and female he created them.

Acts 17- 27 KJV That they should seek the Lord, if haply they might feel after him, and find him, though he be not far from every one of us.

Philippians 4-13 KJV "I can do all things through Christ which strengtheneth me." **Romans 8-28 KJV** And we know that all things work together for good to them that love God, to them who are called according to his purpose.

Chapter 10

Scriptures are the spoken words of God. Apply them into the context of understanding them. However, do not rewrite or change the word/words of God.

You not only are a true champion, victorious and beautiful, you are an imitation of Christ. Nothing gets better than that.

Nothing coming against you, nor any weapon formed. Friends hurting you, they were not ever friends, they wanted you hurt or hurting. Pray over it and release it, move on. God is our comforter, and he is a true friend indeed! It is a shallow person who wants to hurt another. A person who does not have the friendship you have to offer them to you. A taker not a giver and truly if someone does not want you happy or to succeed, how is that a good friendship?

Blow the whistle, toot the horn, you are the child that is born. Be all you can be. You can and you will.

Elan, Stan, nor man made you; God made you. We serve God not man.

We are to be a service to our fellow man with love as Christ loved.

Someone will always try to burst your bubble and cause trouble.

You may even be doing it. You have no reason to condemn yourself. We all make mistakes and were they mistakes?

Did you learn from them? Did you grow from them?

God has forgiven you and forgotten them if you came and confessed them and asked God to forgive them. So, why are you holding onto them?

Start today and start to see the good in them, what good came from them or it.

Be thankful to God for all things. Yes, in loss and trying times, we can be thankful too.

We are not here to meet people's expectations or demands. We do not owe anyone an explanation. The shadow of what they did not fulfill in their lives is not the core for which God has designed you. We are individuals and should treasure and respect one another, just as God has made us individually.

Love surpasses all and with God, we are loved, and God is love.

We come before and to God and confess our sins, and we are to confess to and with one another, but nowhere does it say we are to condemn and judge. We will all stand before God one day and give an account for everything. So, each day we should try and glorify and live for God in accordance with how he wants us to live and be (strive) pleasing unto him.

Putting our best and our all in our affairs (not an affair), our family, spouse, children, job, neighbors, and do and be the best we can.

Even when yes, things are not going well or people are not treating you well.

It certainly is not easy, but God knows, and he does not want his child, son, or daughter hurting.

Cover the offense. Pray and release it to him. God is the answer. He also will provide the answers. So, start seeing God manifest a change in your life, that is a delight. Put down the clothes of what you are hiding from, or in, or even trying to hide. Put on the crown and robe God has for you and walk tall as he has designed for each of us.

We are the apple of his eye. Choose that and embrace it.

Let all guilt and condemnation go. Forgive yourself, forgive others, and quit targeting yourself with darts. It not only will hurt you, but it will also hurt others and your relationship/relationships.

Maybe start with one thing about yourself that is good among many you have and say, thank you Father, for I am strong. Thank you father because I have a lot of love to give- I can teach, I can paint, I can organize, I can, I can. Not I can't. Not, I am worthless. Nothing is worthless. Everything has a purpose and its purpose.

Why would you want to disagree with God? He knew you before you were even born. He says he has hope and a future. That's awesome. He believed now, you, believe. You can do all things with Christ.

Challenge yourself today to no longer condemn yourself. Forgive yourself, putting those things behind and pressing forward. Do not allow condemnation from others. A step in your way to who God has called you to be.

There is a difference when someone speaks, talks to you, and with you.

It is an impartation of experience shared and wisdom.

Wisdom is to be embraced and passed on.

Experience is a shared event. This is appreciation at the forefront by both sides. Enjoy it, learn, and even if not, one day, one moment, it may be something very valuable.

The other judgment is not lifting, nor is it valuable in any form or context.

Dismiss that. When you see harm, or jealousy, or not in line with God, or of God, choose to stand on God's word. Thank them and hold nothing against anyone. Choose your friends wisely.

We are all subjected to change, including our friends, family, and co-workers. Acknowledge them and be respectful of that change, but don't condemn them either. Stay within the boundaries of love and adapt.

Sometimes, you must step back, step away, and now in technology delete. Delete chat and block. Some applies to condemnation. Block-block-block.

God supplies all our needs.

You can start being the best you are by throwing the luggage away you have been carrying filled with rocks inside around. When you release them, the people you are around will see the difference and relationships will improve. You'll be lighter with rocks gone (weight), and happiness and peace will set in. Joy, joy, joy!

A new you, a better you.

Makes no sense to harbor every day something that God does not want you to hold onto. His yoke is light.

Ephesians 5-1 KJV "Be ye therefore followers of God, as dear children."

Colossians 2-13 NIV When you were dead in your sins and in the uncircumcision of your flesh, God made you alive with Christ. He forgave us all our sins.

Thessalonians 5-18 ESV Give thanks in all circumstances; for this is the will of God in Christ Jesus for you.

Timothy 4 2-5 TPT- The Passion Translation-Proclaim the word of God and stand upon it no matter what! Rise to the occasion and preach when it is convenient and when it is not. Preach in the full expression of the Holy Spirit- with wisdom and patience as you instruct and teach the people.

Isaiah 41-10 KJV Fear thou not; for I am with thee; be not dismayed; for I am thy God; I will strengthen thee; yea, I will help thee, yea, I will uphold thee with the right hand of my righteousness.

1 John 4-16 KJV And we have known and believed the love that God hath to us. God is love, and he that dwelleth in love dwelleth in God, and God in him.

Chapter 11

In trying times always remember who our creator is.

We will suffer trials and tribulations, but Jesus died on the cross and suffered.

Do we have any right to complain? God knows our tears and our hurts, and he captures each tear we weep out.

We can also overcome, and it may not be a long process, but God will never forsake you or give you more than you can handle or have strength for.

Hurting and Crying Out

God will be right along with you, and you will feel, love, and laugh again.

With so much that God has for us, and his unconditional love, and by Jesus's blood it is done, finished. It is an amazing gift all of us have been given. Is he your savior?

Don't lose hope-

Don't quit.

You matter!

God loves you and so do I. We are to love one another and lift each other up.

You are special and don't you ever forget that.

Don't let the forecast predict what you do or not do. Call it! Do it!

Cloudy, snow, do not let clouds cast cover over your journey. Even weathering a TUSAMI, you can do it with the Grace of God. Increments, small steps, are better than no steps or disbelief formed. Capture the moment do not be captured by it

Captivation stops and starves the soul, the production. As the saying goes, the sun will shine again. Let God's radiance and light shine down on you and through. You will start shining too.

As it is written, you are more than a conqueror. Conqueror means to subdue, grasp, achieve win, with that being said, you are yes, you are a winner. Anything you see as defeat, our savior has come to experience, overcame, and is victorious. He (Jesus) sits at the right side of heaven, with and along our father God. So debonair, distinguished, and conquered.

Face adversity with gladness. God gives us adversity as well as good times. Always praying with thanksgiving and gratitude. It shall be that nothing on earth shall move me or shatter me with God. All things are possible. What does not work one way may work in another way another day.

Have the courage to believe.

Strength to try.

Faith to believe.

Perseverance to continue in God's promises.

Hope to know God's word is true. Today, yesterday, and forever more.

In continuance, you shall see God's hand and manifestation of God's design in your life.

In his timing not yours.

If God says it is so, then believe it.

It is time to say goodbye to the shadow and embark on what God has called and created.

Psalm 56 8-11 NIV Record my misery list my tears on your scroll are they not in your record?

Then my enemies will turn back

When I call for help

By this I will know that God is for me.

In God, whose word I praise, in the Lord, whose word I praise- In God I trust and am not afraid.

What can man do to me?

Psalm 56-9 KJV: When I cry unto thee, then shall mine enemies turn back: this I know, for God is for me.

Ecclesiastes 7-14 NLT Enjoy prosperity while you can, but when hard times strike, realize that both come from God. Remember that nothing is certain in this life.

Psalm 119-116 KJV Uphold me according unto thy word, that I may live: and let me not be ashamed of my hope.

John 11-40 NIV Then Jesus said, "Did I not tell you that if you believe, you will see, the glory of God?"

Revelation 3-8 KJV I have set before thee an open door, and no man can shut it.

Philippians 4-19 NIV And my God will meet all your needs according to the riches of his glory in Christ Jesus.

Chapter 12

No matter what you are facing, anger, loss, abandonment, even doubt value of yourself (worth; don't beat yourself down). Do not allow thoughts negative or delusional to filter or fester in your mind.

Concentrate on the promises God has given to each one of us.

I can do all things through Christ, who strengthens me.

Nothing is impossible for those who love God.

He has your name on the palm of his hand. He knows how many hairs you have by number.

Swipe to the left any visions or thoughts that are not in alliance with God's teachings or promises.

Yes, it is hard, but you are worth it. You are valuable to God.

Not only do we have the Father (our Father), we have Jesus as our savior, the Son of God, and the Holy Spirit to guide us and make intercession on our behalf to our Father, God.

With that being said, we have the best team on board ever available.

He will lead you on the course and the course you are to be on.

In some, one may encounter events, one after another, which will pelmet you to where you are supposed to be and destined.

Keep your focus and love on God.

You will see the light illuminating and his radiance shining down and out through you.

Take a moment and believe in God. Let the adverse thoughts dispel an exit and watch God fill you with thoughts of you can, you will, and I am with you.

Feed yourself on the thoughts that are true, lovely, and pure. God is, for sure, highly noble. He is true, lovely, and pure.

Tell yourself no one, nothing, will stop, or hinder, or destroy what God has chosen and designed you to be.

Believe and hope in the Lord.

Let his love be your filter. Your source, your rock!! You will rock it.

Most things do not happen instantly, but with God, ALL things are possible!!

Also, some things you think of are drawn into much bigger things than they really are. Dare to envision them in and from God's eyes. God created everything.

You may seek outside help, counseling, church (pastoral assistance/counseling), or a physician, but whatever the circumstances call for, receive them and do NOT act on feelings or emotions. That is the enemy's lies!

Embrace yourself, celebrate yourself. Even talking to yourself from within/inside.

You are a child of God.

You are his son/daughter.

You are wonderful.

You are unique and so made in the image of God.

You can because God says so.

Hurting and Crying Out

You are an achiever- don't think lies are being fed you are not by the deceiver (Satan). Stop those at the onset and know what God has spoken about you and over you.

Do not allow yourself to be moved by the opposition. Nor any force which is out of line and not centered or directed by God.

God opens doors and closes doors. God is the channel in which love flows. Allow an overflow and outpouring of his love.

The hurt is there.

The feelings and emotions of loss and failure are there.

It may feel you have no answers, and it is very cold and dark where you are momentarily. That is when God prevails. He is with you shining his light and his love upon you.

When you are weak, God is strong.

He is your lifeline. Take a hold of that and stand on the solid foundation of what and who our Father is.

Strong, unfailing, consistent, true, loving, and he knows all and sees all.

Hold onto his promises. Let no one or anything tell you differently.

You can, you will, and you shall.

One step at a time.

Try today, right now to see what God has planned and can do.

Think positive thoughts about all things.

God never gives us more than we can handle.

It may not seem right or fair, but God is the answer.

Even if bleak and in a place currently that you do not understand or did, hold steadfast unto him. Set your focus on him. It does <u>NOT</u> matter what man says or has to say, it matters what God says.

He spoke it before you were even born. He knows the plans and the future which God has in store for you and for me.

Abraham and Sara had a child in their golden years. Almost if not always impossible at their ages. However, God spoke it and kept his promise to them.

You need to speak words of faith over yourself and believe God for them.

We don't always get what we want. But, if we try, we get what we need.

Leading to what God has in store for what he, our Father has designed for you.

You may even feel as if you are on an iceberg, floating with no direction, only a dream, but while on that iceberg, God knows you will reach land (your destination). God will be and is with you in everything.

When you do not see, rest in him, keep believing, and focus on him.

Affirm his promises and know you can always count on him.

You will laugh again, dance again, love again.

2 Corinthians 1-20 NIV for all the promises of God in him are yea, and in him Amen, unto the glory of God by us.

Job 17-9 NIV Nevertheless, the righteous will hold to their ways, and those with clean hands will grow stronger.

Philippians 4-13 KJV I can do all things through Christ which strengtheneth me.

Isaiah 49-16 NIV See, I have engraved you on the palms of my hands; your walls are ever before me.

Philippians 4-8 KJV Finally brethren, whatsoever things are honest, whatsoever things are just, whatsoever things are pure, whatsoever things are lovely, whatsoever things are of good report;

if there be any virtue, and if there be any praise, think on these things.

Matthew 28- 20 KJV Teaching them to observe all things what-soever. I have commanded you; and, to. I am with you always, even unto the end of the world. Amen.

Hebrews 4-12 KJV For the word of God is quick, and powerful, and sharper than any two-edged sword, piercing even to the dividing asunder of soul and spirit, and of the joints and marrow, and is a discerner of the thoughts and intents of the heart.

Chapter 13

If you feel (feel) an emotion, thought, or thoughts for a moment that you can't, step back and STOP that thought. God gives you the authority to stand against (what the enemy has come to take/harm).

Nothing is impossible with God or for God.

Take that to the throne. Release it into God's hands, and stand strong, and be of good courage.

Do not take anything out on yourself or be in such despair, you can reach out to get help or counseling.

It does not matter what the world thinks or what other people think. Or what others would think.

If you are hurting, unsure and crying out - **REACH OUT!**

Not only reach out-shout out for the King of Kings, Lord of Lords, Almighty God.

Our Father will be with you always.

God is the way, God-is the answer.

He (God) will be with you and lead you to the doors, yes doors, God, has open for you and all of us.

God says he will lead you in the way you should go.

I will direct your steps.

I have a future for you.

Do not make any decisions based on circumstances or other opinions.

First off, know God directs everything.

It is the enemy who tries to rob, kill, and destroy.

Do not fall or buy into the enemy's attack. Resist him and he shall flee.

Do not let what someone says infect you or have any hold on you or over you.

Everyone has an opinion, just as we all have backtraps. Let it release as the back trap as it is the same. Waste!!

Non-important.

Not only allow it to go- say I will not be moved by it but will move and stand on and by the word of God.

Nothing formed against me shall prosper, EVER!

You are a child of God. God is pleased with you. God loves you. God has beautiful things in store for you.

If you are at a terrible time, there is nothing wrong with hurting or crying.

No one has the power to hurt another to this point, God is power and you can rise above this. You can achieve, you can get someone to help, hear, and listen to you. There is no shame in that.

Just think, if you did, the people left behind would be hurt over a rash decision and it would hurt them deeply.

Should you need to reach out and call someone now, reach the crisis line at either **988** or **1-800-273-8255**

Hurting and Crying Out

God loves you and will never forsake you. You are not alone, as he (God) is always with you. We have a Father, Son, and the Holy Spirit.

Stop and reassess this feeling and make the call to get the help you need. Friends/ friends, family, keep calling, call assessment center, crisis, and get counseling/care to overcome what you are feeling and going through.

Hope- hope that is not deferred.

Rest in God, His peace.

Allow God to take your hand and walk through this moment into what he has promised you.

There is nothing that difficult for God.

Stand strong and be of good courage.

It not only will get better- but it will also be better.

God says he wants us to have life more abundantly.

No lack.

Stand firmly on his promises and his words!

Lead us not into temptation but deliver us from evil for thine (God) is the kingdom, the power, and the glory.

His hand, his way!

Take the step and make the call/calls for a brighter and promised future.

You are important and loved very much!

Some people never go through dark clouds, but we all have our own share. Nothing in life is without purpose. You, my love, are the purpose. Let God's love transcend you into what he has called you to be.

Others have tremendous trials and suffering. The key to this is- not asking why, it is I do not understand, it is not even "I Can't." You can, you shall, and you will succeed.

God gives us what we can handle and never more than enough. God has prepared us for this even before we were born.

He knows the finish too. It is restorations, joy, multiplying your losses, peace, love, and better than before.

All tests have a formula, and if we respond properly (not fleshly) self, self-pity, or absorbed.

You will ace this test. He already has a way.

God is that way.

We can all beam again and have new beginnings, regardless of the circumstances, age, addictions, guilt. We serve an amazing father, and he loves you just as you are. You are pretty special.

Right now, hug yourself and say you are pretty wonderful.

You can do things through Christ, who strengthens you.

Make that call. Get help have a grand today and a wonderful tomorrow.

Let all holding you loose and smile.

We love you.

If you are in a state of despondency, call the hotline or crisis number for the state you are in. They will stay with you and assist you in managing the issues bothering you at present.

Sometimes, medicine and good counseling can rectify the root cause of an alarm.

Do not beat yourself up over this. Help is available to everyone.

God is our provider, and he supplies all our needs daily. Nothing is too difficult that you can't do or overcome. Recognize it and seek help. You will be very happy you did, and your loved ones will be too.

God is our healer and our comforter.

Luke 10-19 KJV Behold, I give unto you power to tread on serpents and scorpions, and over the enemy; and nothing shall any means hurt you.

Psalm 145-3 KJV Great is the Lord, and greatly to be praised. And his greatness is unsearchable. One generation shall praise thy works to another. And shall declare thy mighty acts.

John 14-6 KJV Jesus saith unto him, I am the way, the truth, and the life; no man cometh unto the Father, but by me.

Jerimiah 29-11 NIV For I know the plans I have for you, declares the Lord, plans to prosper you and not to harm you, plans to give you hope and a future.

Deuteronomy 31-8 KJV And the Lord, he it is that doth go before thee, he will be with thee, he will not fail thee, neither forsake thee, fear not, neither be dismayed.

Proverbs 13-12 KJV Hope deferred maketh the heart sick; But when the desire cometh, it is a tree of life.

Psalm 33 20-22 NIV We wait in hope for the Lord; he is our shield. In him our hearts rejoice, for we trust in his holy name. May your unfailing love be with us, Lord, even as we put our hope in you.

1 Corinthians 10-13 NIV No temptation has overtaken you except what is common to mankind. And God is faithful; he will not let you be tempted beyond what you can bear. But when you are tempted, he will also provide a way out so that you can endure it.

Chapter 14

If someone is pressing in on you and you have to take a stand to defend every little thing or comment on social media, step back for a moment and ask yourself, why?

Who is it that you are correcting or blasting?

Does it matter what someone says or their opinion of you?

We serve or should be God.

Does God go around posting on social media platforms?

No!

Does God go on television or in a rag magazine and write stories that are not true? Or even if they are true?

No!

You are popular or not, it does not matter. That is the flesh, ego, pride.

Let it go.

God is with the brokenhearted.

God avenges, not man.

God is the only real celebrity.

Forget it, pray over it, forgive it and them. Everyone of everything.

It really is not important, nor does it elevate you in any shape or form.

Instead of fighting with opinions, angst (anger), doubt, or lack, turn (surrender) it all over and unto God. Completely, not part.

Pray overall and even if hurting, pray as it releases all (formed) yes, formed. Nothing is against you. God is for you, today, tomorrow, and forever more.

Do not close doors you have not opened. Let God open them and you walk through them and in them with Purpose and Destination.

Hurting and Crying Out

You are never alone, and you are never defeated. God so loved the world that he gave his only begotten son so that we would have life more abundantly.

Cast, casting all your cares on him.

What a great father.

Don't be downcast, broken, or filled with I can't.

Stop! Stop thinking of-and-on yourself!!

It is of the flesh, the enemy's attack on you. The enemy attacks us on our weaknesses and tries to prevail and achieve to rob, steal, kill, and destroy. When you have something great in front of you, he comes in to try and deceive you. If he can throw something in and try to deceive you then he succeeds. Let me tell you, he is a liar. Believe in yourself and stand firm on the written word.

Dependent solely on God to supply all your needs. The enemy will flee.

Nowhere does it say life will be a carousel and no trials or disruptions.

I say disruptions as they are. God's strength prevails and he says, my grace is sufficient for you. God is working on these before you even experience them. It is up to us to work along with; so, in love, trust (no doubting). Full dependency upon our heavenly father results in a joyful heart, peace, and fulfillment of his promises.

Not controlling God with your way, your ways, your wants.

Praying for healing, prosperity, happiness, and dreams, to name a few, he is and will do all things. It is his will be done. In his timing.

As stated in a previous chapter, it is by his ways, his will. It can be more than you ever imagined that he blesses you with. God wants to bless you. Everything belongs to God. Our longings are God's longings too. He looks down upon you and thinks of you always. You are his child, and he loves you very much. His ways and his thoughts are higher than ours.

Allow yourself the privileged dreams and our visions. The privilege to pray to God.

Asking for discernment in your decisions, dreams, and in everything.

Always being kind to one another. Regardless of if they are being kind to you or not.

That weight is not meant for you to carry. Release it and let it go.

It does not matter what anyone says. Be it a celebrity, politician, artist, musician, author, gymnast, businessman or woman. We are all children of God. He always watches over us.

Nothing in this world is important to lose one night's sleep over what someone says or thinks.

Not one night over debt or another that is taking hold of you. That is pride and things will work themselves out.

Ride the storm/storms out. Rest in God.

Losses, business, marriage, other, God, will provide a way.

It does not say that it will not hurt. It does. It hurts to the very core, but centered is God, Christ, and the Holy Spirit. They know you're hurt. God says he carries you in the storms. He does watch the amazing things that he does and how you will succeed and get through them.

You are getting better and better every day. See yourself so.

God is God. You are not God. You did not create the world and everything in it.

God did. Nor did you get things by chance. God is solid and he provides all things.

You can do nothing apart from God.

He is making you stronger so you Can!

Once you take yourself out of focus and see God as your provider, you will see incredible changes, possibilities that you have put limitations on.

You will see business picking up or expanding. Or possibly a new business. You may have lost a spouse/companion or connection, but God has reconnection, so all is possible with God.

Walk forward and continue to grow. Do not let any opposition overpower, take, or destroy you. You will make it.

You will see the changes, meant for your good, to emerge.

Trust in God and God's timing.

Even if people say it's taking too long. God is the author and the finisher.

Release that into when it is time, it will be. Continue to do what you were called to do, and let God perfect you and all in it to his design for you.

Did you create the earth, the sea, the mountains, trees, life??

God knows what he is doing.

Start by enjoying and embracing yourself and God and know the love he has for you and watch how amazing he truly is.

When you open your eyes and your heart, you will be astounded.

You can start now-delete, block, step away from the inboxes, comment on the social cycle. You need no opinion. God's thoughts are higher than our thoughts.

People who care about you are ones whose opinions you may want to listen to, uplifting, encouraging, and supportive. Someone who is not critical, jealous, or has an agenda of their own.

Friends are to be as iron sharpens iron. Distinguish that.

Some may walk away, be sour, hurt you, be envious, think of themselves better, or be selfish, but they are not friends in any form. It could even be 5-10 years later, and it manifests itself and you see this. It could even be several events ongoing at the same time. It is ok and you will see this as a present. Yes, present. Open it, look to the sky and let it fly. You are not here to please them. Change for them. You are going ahead into what God has in store for you- that they are jealous of. Acknowledge that and release it.

They tell you how you should be and do things, but it is your dream and your vision.

God is moving them so he can prepare you for your journey and the next step/promotion.

You will make new friends.

God says: For I know the plans I have for you!

Work towards your dream/dreams, goals and thank God always!

You may pray this prayer.

Help me, to rest in you Lord.

Help me to see through.

I know right now I feel it's too much for me to bare,

But I know it is you that cares.

I may not see a way,

But I know you are the way.

Help me to stand strong,

When all things are going wrong.

Right now, I change my view

And not act on feelings.

I know in my heart you are the reason.

Thank you for your love and standing with me, Setting me free from adversity.

I will step up to your promises and see hope, for my tomorrow.

Today, Yahweh Amen.

Put away feelings and a wrong mindset.

Reach out now and make that call for help. Pursue the plans God has for you.

You can and are a winner.

You can and will be victorious.

You are loved, so loved.

1 John 2- 15 KJV Love not the world, neither the things that are in the world. If any man love the world, the love of the Father is not in him.

Psalm 34 18-22 KJV The Lord is nigh unto them that are of a broken heart; and saveth such as be of a contrite spirit. Many are the afflictions of the righteous; But the Lord delivereth him out of them all. He keepeth all his bones; Not one of them is broken.

Romans 12 19-21 NIV Do not take revenge, my dear friends, but leave room for God's wrath, for it is written: It is mine to avenge: I will repay; says the Lord. On the contrary: If your enemy is hungry, feed him, if he is thirsty, give him something to drink.

James 4-7 KJV Submit yourselves therefore to God; Resist the devil, and he will flee from you.

Psalms 28-7 KJV The Lord is my strength and my shield, my heart trusted in him, and I am helped: therefore, my heart greatly rejoiceth; and with my song will I praise him.

Proverbs 3 5-6 KJV Trust in the Lord with all thine heart; and lean not unto thine own understanding; In all thy ways acknowledge him, and he shall direct thy paths.

Nahum 1-7 KJV The Lord is good, A strong hold in the day of trouble; and he knoweth them that trust in him.

John 15-5 NIV "I am the vine; you are the branches. If you remain in me, and I in you, you will bear much fruit; apart from me you can do nothing."

Lamentations 3 25- 26 KJV "The Lord is good unto them that wait for him, to the soul that seeketh him. It is good that a man should both hope and quietly wait for the salvation of the Lord."

John 16 –13 ESV When the Spirit of truth comes, he will guide you into all of the truth, for he will not speak on his own authority, but whatever he hears he will speak, and he will declare to you the things that are to come.

John 16-33 KJV These things I have spoken unto you, that in me ye might have peace. In the world ye shall have tribulation; but be of good cheer; I have overcome the world.

Chapter 15

Tomorrows may never evolve, so embrace today. Quit putting off what you were called and designed for you to a later date. More than likely, we will be blessed with a tomorrow. Don't take anything for granted.

Everything is a gift from God, all lives matter to God and others.

You have done nothing or ever could without God.

It is flagrant and insulting to believe or say, I did it myself.

No, my friend, you did not do it without the Lord.

He has been with you all the way and in everything.

Do the best you can and be the best you can in all things today.

Not only read the word of God, listen to the word of God.

We can't mold (form) him into what we want or the outcome of certain circumstances.

Hurting and Crying Out

We are to come boldly to the throne and make our requests known. Putting them there with thanksgiving.

In all things, acknowledge God.

It is not our way or ways.

It is God's will. God's will be done.

His timing.

You may be called, have a gift (or gifts) that God has given (placed) inside of you- for a purpose- his purpose!

Do not ever see it as you did it, control it, as you are not higher than God.

You can do nothing without God or by the power of God. It is all within his control and his creation.

You must surrender your ways to envelop together(blend) to his. He will use your gifts and define your purpose.

Do not be afraid or be in or of fear.

Do it with reverence and love towards him.

It is easy to cop out, quit, fold up, but one foot in front of the other leaning on God, will be a step you will never regret.

Think of all the blessings and happiness you have had. See these and remember them now and count them as all joy!

He never left you and you are not alone. God will never leave you.

You are strong.

You can do all things you were and are created to do!

Including-adversity We will say tomorrow:

For tomorrows are here for us and generation to generation. Nothing has not that has not and is not being lived from before and to current. Stand strong in the Lord. Let God be your avenger.

You are doing and moving towards your calling. You may have suffered, loss, health, finances, addictions, betrayal, but you have gone through. God will never leave you. You can go through now too.

There is nothing to ever cause such despair to end one's life or throw in the towel.

Nothing!

You may have health issues. Say cancer- a poison- do not let the poison become you.

Embrace it and determine yourself to be made whole- that you will embrace each day with joy and let God use you as you watch the days unfold toward your healing.

Nothing is impossible with God. Nor is there anything that should ever take hold or root that destroys who God made you to be. Robbing you of the day and days ahead. Being strong and of good courage. Love and enjoying the day ahead is what you should allow to root and be everything that God has called you to be. Not robbing you of anything that would take from your strength or healing.

With finances, finances are subject to change. They are not meant to establish your life.

No monetary value things (possessions) hold nor do they mean anything. All can be taken in an instant, and all can be replaced, taken, or lost.

God supplies all our needs.

Are you a giver or a taker?

Do you consider yourself above everyone?

We are all the children of God. No one is better than you and you are not better than anyone else. We all have something and are someone.

Hurting and Crying Out

Do not let money- or any other become your idol, your worth, your value. Set your eyes on God. Declare his promises. He will heal you, by his stripes, you are healed. He came so we would have life more abundantly.

Set your eyes on God.

Things can change and let your day be your tomorrow. Live it joyfully and watch the day turn into radiance. In other words, live for today and see tomorrow be brighter and better.

The key to happiness everyone asks is: The decision to be happy.

Choose it and watch how amazing and magnificent God works and is.

We are not promised tomorrow. God promises us eternal life in his kingdom. If we repent and accept Jesus as our personal savior and confess our sins.

We are the righteousness of God, by Christ, who credits our account by his blood, which God sees us as blameless.

The Armor of God.

It will protect you in every way.

Allow God to lead you to where God wants you.

Don't try to be God.

He not only will make a way, but God is also the way!

By Jesus' death, there is no more sickness, lack, or despair, we are overcomers by his death.

It is the enemy's attack to interfere with the plans God has for you, so stand on the solid rock. God's foundation.

Time is a gift; life is a gift. You are a present. A special present in the presence.

Do not take things or life for granted.

God is a gift; Jesus is a gift. It is a privilege to worship, honor, and love them.

He gives us free will free thoughts. Choose wisely. Choose life!!

These thoughts, the feelings, the angst, all shall/will pass.

Circle yourself with today. Joy, peace, our heavenly father and Son. Let the Holy Spirit make intercession on your behalf. Pray.

Do not become crippled or perplexed by an attack from the enemy.

You may have something defined as depression, anxiety, or other. With a therapist and proper care and treatment you can become the child God has called you to be. Even with medication, a good support system you can do all things and achieve.

Do not be defined by a condition. Depression, adultery, addiction, gossiping, whatever may pop up, allow the entrance of God to fill you.

Accept Jesus as your savior and let the redeemed of the Lord say so. Declare victory and healing over yourself.

You will-you can- start now, today.

Your today is the possibility of your tomorrow.

Declare you will not hurt any longer and you will see brighter days.

Declare there is no sickness, lack, brokenness, by the blood of Jesus-he says so!

Speak words of grace-let God's power shine in and out through you. You will have life more abundantly. The things we go through are temporal. God promises to restore the broken and hurting. God will not give us any more than you or I can bear. So, you are equipped to handle this with God and outside help. Depending on the urgency and extreme of the state or despair that you are in. God has spoken.

Let his words fill you and give life to you. God loves you unconditionally.

You can find joy and peace in <u>all</u> circumstances.

It is the key to how you respond to it that makes the total difference.

Dare to dream, believe, and hope-

You shall see it in your today's-

I wish I could reach out and hug you and tell you that you are so special and that these things will truly pass, but my words are with you and God's words are promises founded and planted firmly on the rock. Embrace them and God.

Hebrews 4-16 KJV Let us therefore come boldly unto the throne of grace, that we may obtain mercy, and find grace to help in time of need.

Isaiah 41-10 KJV Fear thou not; for I am with thee; be not dismayed, for I am God, I will strengthen thee; yea, I will help thee; yea, I will uphold thee with the right hand.

Philippians 4-19 KJV But my God shall supply all your need according to his riches in glory by Christ Jesus.

John 1 12-13 NIV Yet to all who did receive him, to those who believe in his name, he gave the right to become children of God-children born not of natural

descent, nor of human decision, or a husband's will, but born of God. We are all children of God.

Luke 1-37 KJV "For with God nothing shall be impossible."

Joshua 1-9 KJV Have not, I commanded thee? Be strong and of a good courage; be not afraid, neither be thou dismayed, for the Lord thy God is with thee.

Chapter 16

To much baggage, not feeling worthy?

Who gave you that idea?

Everyone has something. If they don't, they are less than honest. You also are not defined by your baggage either. It is events that you went through and succeeded, as there is no such thing as failure. The only thing we can fail at is the fact we do not try or give things our attention or the best we have to give.

We all have stuff.

We all go to places. Pits- broken dreams, loss-divorce-addictions-loneliness-and on and on.

Sometimes, we are our own worst enemies. Expecting to much or having no drive or direction.

Excuses!

Acknowledge them whether you chose them freely or fell into them. It is a part of you and your journey.

Nothing is wasted or a waste. You went through them or are going through them. Maybe some are mistakes; however, hopefully, we learn, are learning, we grow, we stretch, we mature, and better ourselves. We can be a blessing or help someone with what we know or have learned. So, by all means acknowledge it and accept it as it is. Do not blame yourself, carry it around and let it fester, as it stops you from being the person God created you to be.

Take time to know what God says about it.

You are who God says you are.

His precious son or daughter.

No one has a right to make you conform to their standards or judge you.

Be thankful for all things, count it as all joy.

Embrace it and accept it.

Forgive everything, as stated before, even covering them or their issues. You will be grateful that you did.

Hurting and Crying Out

God sees our pain.

God knows our pain.

God is good and restores all that is lost.

It is not easy, nor is it fun, but the course you run during it and who your partner/partners are (Father, Son, and Holy Spirit) outweigh anything you are going through or currently in.

Don't you define yourself by the baggage.

Don't take it out and keep repacking it either.

Grab it, shake it, nicely put it aside, (look at it/all) cry, shout at it, hug it, fold it nicely (accept), lay aside. Put them together neatly (embrace, forgive) and start putting it in the suitcase box to pack away. (Forgive put away) when all is in (next vacation, moving, relationship, etc.), look at it, thank God.

You have it, you succeeded at going through and it is time to move forward now into better things. Each of us has something.

A loss, accept it, as the increase is on its way.

Your loss is not a loss. You had it or someone for a time and you and they brought moments of love and joy to each other. Situations, circumstances evolved, finances, adultery, death, immaturity, self, greed, whatever it may be, but there is something in and from both. A blessing/ blessing from. Hold onto that.

It is not a weight. You will bloom again.

We can't control our lives, events, or circumstances, but how we respond to them we can. Allow God to move you and his hand each moment, that the step you take, you will see things get better and better each day.

Cheating, an affair, someone cheated on you; don't condemn them for their decision or yourself. It is not you they cheated on. They cheated on themselves. There are many reasons for looking for something they don't even know or are aware of. A good fling. Something to get away with. Something we don't (so they say) give them, or we bring money, and things. Thinking the grass is greener on the other side. False promises. Brokenness inside. It is a careless decision that is made. It is not your fault or even another's they cheated.

Such as you don't have time, they are bored, there is no laughter, you won't do this or that, age, medical condition, not able to perform any longer, appetite for, excuse after excuse. It is not that person's fault. It is a fleshly desire, which is love and the connection to; created by God in love, between and joined by two people in love, and love for one another and between one another. It is not a sporting event.

There are also alternatives before stepping out and cheating two people may share things together and explore alternatives. If there is a pause or hold on sexual interactions. There is no excuse for disappearing or cheating spouse. These are things you must take heed of as they are not of God or condoned by God.

This, however, is not an alternative to lose hope or quit either.

God says; Put all your trust in me, lean not in your own understanding. My ways are higher than your ways, and my thoughts, higher than your thoughts.

If it has gotten to a place where you are going/thinking of ending the relationship, first and foremost, ask:

Is it just a lustful feeling?

Is it based on feelings alone? Or more so, just yourself?

Remember you have someone too, your wife, your husband. The other person may have someone too. There is a lot to contend with. It is a very sticky situation to become involved in for a few moments of pleasure or not. Think about it before you succumb to temptation.

Seek out marriage counseling. Your church pastor. An addiction facility. First and foremost, seek your partner. Love them enough to come to them to talk. Care about them and their feelings. If anything, try to work these things out together if you can. Everything deserves an effort and not accusations, abandonment, and destruction for a moment and or because something appears to be better. People are a case of their own.

We need to lift others; iron sharpens iron.

Not isolate us unto our own judgments. He this, she this, he, she that.

It says neither Greek or Jew, rich or poor, slave or free.

Judgments!

Who are you to pass judgment or to judge me, or I you? Who are you because you have a rough day thwarting your opinion (yes, opinion) of me? Is it Godly or justified? Is it love, is it kind? No, it is downright about pride and self. Have you remotely thought about what they are going through? Do you make judgments without inquiring or inquiries? What about if that person was hurting so much inside, "you" are the person who with your opinion formed in the heat of a moment, either added to that person's last thread (holding on by) and you pushed that button?

Sometimes, instead of honoring God and obeying (obediently follow), we act as if we are God. God so loved us he sent his Son (Jesus) so we could be forgiven for our sins. What a gift, what a privilege to be loved. He so loved the world and everyone in it.

Who are you to decide who can love and be loved?

Your tomorrow may be brighter if you cast your love out today for your fellow man.

Love is kind never wanting its own.

Take a step forward to possess all of God's promises.

He restores the brokenhearted and lost. God never leaves us or forsakes us.

Yes, even people who hurt us, we are to pray for and over them. Even covering them. You can't keep hurting over affliction caused by others. Intentional or not. Even if they think they are better and have no feelings except those of themselves or gain.

Allow yourself to be free and choose the channel in which God flows. He is wonderful and full of love.

A relationship can be salvaged. There is hope.

Cheating can be forgiven or forgotten; it is the steps you choose to take. However, it is the best in everything to put God in all. He makes sure when you stumble you will not fall.

1 Corinthians 13-4 NIV Love is patient, love is kind. It does not envy, it does not boast, it is not proud.

Deuteronomy 30-3 NIV Then the Lord your God will restore your fortune and have compassion on you and gather you again from all the nations where he scattered you.

Acts 17 24-28 KJV "The God, who made the world and everything in it is the Lord of heaven and earth and does not live in temples built by hands; And he is not served by human hands as if he needed anything, because he himself gives all men life and breath and everything else."

Chapter 17

Crying and hurting have many forms.

The world was created by God. Our creator.

God is just, beautiful and amazing.

It is incredible to even fathom all God created.

Just being thankful for flowers, love (emotions), colors, seas, trees, horses, children, many things. He, God, our father created. (In 7 days) on the 7th day, God completed all his work and he rested. Could you do any of those things in 7 days? It's miraculous. Jesus to come so that we could have life more abundantly. That God so loved the world he gave his only begotten Son (Jesus) that whoever believes in him shall not perish but have everlasting life. What a gift! What Life!

Paul went through many things and continued to stand and remain strong. He was downcast, broken, hurting, and he asked God to take away his thorn. God replied, my grace is sufficient for you. God is with us! Paul asked again, and God responded my grace is sufficient. Do not make things or allow things to become too much for you, let God's grace be sufficient for you too.

Your dreams, your visions, have no blocks. No limitations. God is the Master Creator. You can do <u>all</u> things. With God, in God. All things!

The enemy attacks and uses the things God has designed to promote you into his design and calling he established for you. Be not discouraged. It shall pass. Feelings can become strong (Satan comes to Steal, Kill, Rob, and Destroy). Put on the full armor of God and withstand his attack. Go to God, seek wisdom, pray, change those thoughts, and try to hold onto pure thoughts.

Scream, shout, cry if you must, but do not give up, give in, or quit.

Neither try to repay someone for hurting you. Pray for them instead.

We have God's promises, God's love, and the Son Jesus, who died for our sins.

Recognize that, accept Jesus as your savior and accept by his blood that there is no longer lack.

Situations and circumstances are temporary, but God is eternal. That says a lot.

You can overcome obstacles and adversities as the power of God can change things in an instant.

See this. Dream big, hope big.

Start somewhere.

Age, race, weight, disabilities, finances, education have no limitations. It is the limits you place on yourself.

We can do all things by Christ who strengthens us.

Believe this.

Listen to Christian sermons, watch TV, read, dance, sing, worship, laugh, pray, hug someone, enjoy all God has given you and called you to be.

If you get your mind off yourself and let God take care of you and your needs. You will see amazingly how wonderful our father is.

Be grateful for everything.

The good and the bad. For situations, family, friends, neighbors, and everything each has added to you not just hurt and taken.

Allow God to be the baker and see all he can do with you. Surrender yourself unto him.

As Emeril says Bam- our father says Bam- it is good.

You are good-

You are someone-

You can do great things you can because God says you can.

Life presents many things to all of us good and bad, but in all things, the sun shines. We are not of this world we are just passing through and in it.

Glory to God that we may have such a privilege to know him.

Do you know him?

The journey (yes, journey) we are each on should be along with him, God.

It can be so amazing and rewarding. Love, peace and joy.

Who does not want that?

Hurting and Crying Out

Yes, things are hard.

Yes, they hurt.

Some, more than others.

God is the author and the finisher.

There are people out there going through much more than some of what seem to believe that they can't, called the, I cannot.

Look up to our savior Jesus, who gave up his life for you and me, and see how his suffering, "we" have eternal life. We have no lack.

Your options are great, and God promises us everlasting life.

He, God, heals the brokenhearted.

Seek the Lord and you will not be disappointed.

Be strong and of good courage.

What you can't do on your own, God can.

You are not weak.

It matters nothing that anyone says if it means you settle and quit.

Break those negative thoughts and strongholds.

Start with good thoughts good memories, replace each negative with a positive, even add a positive.

Soon you will start seeing a new outlook, a new vision, and what God has called you to be.

That is:

A son, a daughter of God!

2 Thessalonians 1-6 KJV God is just: He will pay back trouble to those who trouble you.

2 Corinthians 12-7 KJV And lest I should be exalted above measure through the abundance of the revelations, there was given me a thorn in the flesh, the messenger of Satan to buffet me, lest I should be exalted above measure.

1 John 3-2 KJV "Beloved, now are we the sons of God, and it doth not yet appear what we shall be: but we know that, when he shall appear, we shall be like him; for we shall see him as he is."

Hebrews 12-2 NIV Looking unto Jesus the author and finisher of our faith, who for the joy that was set before him endured the cross, despising the shame, and is set down at the right hand of the throne of God.

Psalm 147-3 ESV He heals the broken hearted and binds up their wounds.

Chapter 18

In starting this, we need to reflect on God and his calling.

What is it that brought you to this despair? Can you pinpoint it and immediately deal with it?

Speak up and speak out.

Tell someone. Tell another, and keep going as you will get the help, counseling, assistance that you need.

God says:

Seek: You shall find.

Knock: I will answer.

Ask: You will receive.

Look, recognize, appreciate, and be thankful to God for everything.

Being grateful you are not lacking.

Being grateful, you are around good people, family, and are blessed not only with them but also with a circle of close friends.

Grateful you can get out from underneath yourself and be absorbed with yourself and help or lift another.

Opportunities arise every day.

Sometimes, it is as if you are having a glass full of the best wine. Drinking it but not observing the wonderful color or aroma of your environment or of the fine flavor of the people surrounding you.

It is gulped down or drank with no recognition of thanksgiving or even clarity.

It is taken for granted.

Whether it be a fine wine or a glass of apple juice- look, recognize, appreciate, and be thankful to God for everyone and everything.

Sometimes, it is not just about you, but the choice to rise above yourself and do something for someone else.

A mentor, coach, friend, and even caretaker. Lots of children out are in broken homes, they need love, someone to care for them and most of all quite possibly, need you.

You, my dear, are special and do have a lot to give, be and do yet.

Weigh the possibilities and see all God has in store for you.

Don't say no to a yes. Do your best, let God do the rest and take care of the rest.

There are no limitations, only the limitations you put and place on yourself. There are no limits to what you can do or be -only the limits you place on yourself to <u>not</u> see.

It is there in front of you- hope, brightness, love, and peace. Run and grab it and hold onto the future God has formed for you.

Enjoying all and yes, everything.

Maybe read the story of Job.

It is a tremendous story and even a read me again, as each differs and emerges into a wonderful ending for Job.

Plus, it enlightens about self and where you were (self) when I created the start of the universe. God is speaking. God is so right.

Who are we to guess his creation? Each intricate part of what God created is phenomenal, unique, and masterful.

Life is a gift. Appreciate it and embrace it.

Let the only music- God and God's word filter into your core.

Step back stand out.

Don't ever quit. Hang on and it will get better and better.

Dream of a dream and go for it.

You can be the epitome and master success dare to believe and let God be your captain, your father.

You may or may not have faced things before now which has brought you here, but those things then before you did fight through- God intercedes and is with us always in all things. You went through it or multiple.

You made it.

I repeat, you made it!

This you will too.

Hold onto that and know it is a fleeting moment of angst that shall pass.

It will be better and brighter.

Do not let a second choose for you.

What is a permanent decision and one you cannot reverse?

You are special, you are wanted, and you are needed.

Remember that!

There is no shame in asking, seeking, or reaching out for help.

Even in recovery, it is a process. It's a road worth traveling.

Hurting and Crying Out

Sometimes, even on a road one must travel several times. However, that road has some beauty while on it. It is you driving down it and enjoying yourself in the midst of it. The journey to a wonderful destination.

God empowers us and is full of love and compassion. Let God be your fuel. Energized in success and being successful. God is not condemning or is of condemnation.

God sees all that we are going through, and he makes a way. Receive this wholeheartedly as he, God, is the way, the only way! He, God, is the vine and we are the branches. His vitality, life, and love are feeding us. Like the vine, he is rooted. Firm, strong, living. Be strengthened by his immeasurable strength.

Let go of thinking of you, want, control, and trust in him.

We are not responsible for a person or people's actions. Unkind treatment. Their words or their actions. We are responsible for how we are responding and our responses. Godly-like conduct and infusion of the passion and love we have for Christ.

If they, others continue to strike and hurt it takes root and they (you gave them) consider that they have power/control over you.

If you find yourself in the midst of this stop!

Breathe.

One, you have the power by Christ to stand firm and affirm you love them, appreciate them, respect them, treasure them as friends, but you will no longer be beaten down by them.

Call it change. It is a change and a time when you honestly make that change.

Change yourself by seeing that you are loved and whole.

A person of value, meaning, and strength.

No more advocates for being manipulated and abused.

You need to identify who you are in Christ.

Identify now what is holding onto you. Write it down.

Is what you are looking at God?

Did it come from God?

Is it or has it been "taught" in or by your family?

Does it apply to you?

Or did it just take root? Allowance to enter by you?

Planted?

You see, your plant it can't grow without the proper seed, soil, water nurturing, sun, or shade. When planted properly, it grows into something beautiful and that is you. Sunshine!

A rose, blossom, an orchid, something very structured.

On the other hand, someone planting their values sometimes passes off dry rot, thorns, briars. Strongholds. Not so pretty.

It isn't that they don't care or love you; it is because they don't know the difference, or they are hurt, bitter, lost.

Don't condemn them or put yourself in a perpetual place or position of agony you take on for life.

It will take work and effort on your part.

You can do it.

What you write down-review it and know- God knows.

He has your name in the palm of his hand.

What is a negative write besides it a positive? I would say two if you can, but try one and then add your positive.

I am a child of God. I can do all things it is God who strengthens me.

Not by power or might but by my spirit you can succeed.

Nothing formed against me shall prosper.

Hurting and Crying Out

I am the head not the tail.

They say in life rain must fall and it is not so bad if you see the positive. When it rains it is God's blessings be poured on us.

It cools us off, it allows some productivity inside and out, it bathes the birds and animals, it lets trees and flowers drink and bloom, it soothes the earth, lets the grass grow so animals can graze.

It provides us with water, so it has a lot of positives.

I can't it's raining, oh, sorry it's wet outside, I don't want my hair wet. It can wait. It makes me feel down and dreary.

All these have I attached to them.

It's your course, your decision-choose the right positive.

Each day is a gift.

You are a gift.

Even in health, or abuse, there is help outside there.

If you feel threatened, lost, or without hope- go to a school counselor- a therapist, friends, neighbors, a doctor/physician start somewhere. A pastor, the police- Stand Tall, be bold and courageous!

How you respond to your circumstances is a huge part. Do not react with shouting, anger, or physical contact.

Try to separate remove yourself from the abuse or attack.

Not provoking or fueling.

A cat that does not want to be held will scratch and claw its way down and force release. No one can control (make someone love you) or hold it if it wants down.

It is the same in and with people you can't control anything or anyone making them forcing them.

Same in love.

Can't force someone to love you.

Counseling in relationships is therapeutic and is an option to explore.

So is talking to each other with respect and hearing what each of you need and working towards that goal, one step at a time. One not ten.

God supplies all our needs daily!

Also growing together. (There are many seasons in our lives). - Changes!

Supporting each other and encouraging growth. Each other, not one person.

Loving them to know God has a purpose and you will be there for one another. Reaching out, giving.

Sometimes, it just must end or be ended, so we must accept, adapt, love (forgive), and be thankful for the time God graced us with them. Even when it is one-sided and you can't be friends.

Life does not stop or end without them.

God knows and he already has a new door, a new chapter for you and them.

Let the eagle go- soar, rise above, and fly free.

God is mighty and will cover you underneath his wings. - with comfort and protection. Always forever always.

Jeremiah 29-11 KJV "For I know the plans I have for you; declares the Lord, plans to prosper you and not to harm you, plans to give you hope and a future."

2 Timothy 3-16 KJV All scripture is given by inspiration of God, and is profitable for doctrine, for reproof, for correction, for instruction in righteousness.

Isaiah 41-10 NIV So do not fear, for I am with you; do not be dismayed, for I am your God. I will strengthen you and help you;

with my righteous right hand.

Daniel 10-19 KJV And said, O man greatly beloved, fear not; peace be unto thee, be strong. Yea be strong. And when he had spoken unto me, I was strengthened, and said, Let my lord speak, for thou hast strengthened me.

Joshua 1-9 KJV Have not I commanded thee? Be strong and of good courage, be

not afraid, neither be thou dismayed for the Lord thy God is with thee whithersoever thou goest.

Chapter 19

Health issues may render you at a loss or an understanding of.

Cancer, why me? Facing feelings of and certainly asking all questions concerning what you are lacking in knowledge of. Address everyone you want to ask: oncologist, physician, psychiatrist, everyone. Let no door be not turned and walk through boldly. Even getting more than one opinion.

You may have a statistic, but God is, and God can.

You must be strong, healthy, whole in the midst of this.

Accidents that cause impairments and being disabled, ask and seek.

Seeing how to adapt, improve, improvise, recover, or complete healing. Every transition has a timing to it. Place them into our Father's hands and let him, God work in and through you. God is divine.

God's will-God's timing.

By his stripes, we are healed.

Don't be discouraged, be encouraged.

No one wants to suffer or be in pain. Pain of any kind.

No one wants to be disabled.

No one wants to be lost.

The enemy wants to Rob, kill, and destroy.

Do not allow an illness (poison) to make you a poison or to be poisoned.

Stand up and fight it.

Be strong.

Declare it by God, through God, and with God.

Let each day bring you and fill you with joy.

In the garden of Eden, it was established by the deception of Satan, telling Eve the fruit was just fine to eat. In fact, making it intoxicating. Feeding ourselves lies and illusions does not promote anything.

Feeding on the word of God and standing affirmative to God's words and promises and knowing he is the best if the best you or I will ever have.

The Rock, the creator, the master, the carpenter, the father.

Solid. Not divided.

The doctor gives you a prognosis. You are hurting, but in this you have options. You sit quietly and weigh them. Hopefully, I will turn to God and consult and pray over all of them.

God is with you not just in this moment but right along with you, side by side, in all of it.

Making a choice to wait on God, all directions will be achieved by following our heavenly fathers' wisdom and his designed course.

Do not give in and quit. Become bitter or discouraged.

We can do all things as <u>God</u> strengthens us.

To worry or fear takes away the strength you need to heal, the energy you need to resist and use for and towards healing. It raises your blood pressure.

In the Valley, God is there too.

He walks with you and talks to you. Dare to listen and heed his advice.

We are not designed to heed other people's judgments, opinions, pointed fingers, ridicule, unkindness, as it is not God's design or promises.

When someone makes fun of a disability or difference, it is not only most unkind and hurtful, but one must know they are ignorant in theory.

Immature, not knowing God's word or his promises.

Do not be offended or allow it to soak into who you are and were designed to be by God.

We can enlighten them or ignore them, but it is up to them to receive.

It is up to you to achieve.

To know God's word-his promises-and Jesus as your personal savior.

Hurting people hurt others.

Jealousy is another-greed, lack of faith, all kinds emerge during this-but we should not lose our peace over it by reacting with anger.

Most importantly, we should never be so caught up in ourselves that we place our all into it. That is because we erred or because we don't meet someone's standards, we are nothing. We are worthless. Who are you listening to?

That is a lie!

It is the enemy's attack for not wanting us to have a relationship with God-

O have what God has called you to do-

And placed in your life to attain- gifts and talents.

No one has any right to belittle you. Do not let it take root.

God so loved the world that he gave his only begotten son, Jesus-that we would have life <u>more abundantly</u>!

That says it.

It has been spoken.

Declare it over your life now.

From health, finances, business, family, the throws of disruptions enter (yes, they are disrupting/disruptions).

Nothing is permanent and is subject to change. The responses and your actions can be that which is directed by God and our conductor-or they can be that which are negative-add more to adverse responses, and ultimately diffuse, connection/connections. All things work together for good to those who love God.

Where you do not see a way-

He, God, is the way!

Nothing comes instantly. With a pure heart, willingness, and knowing Christ as your personal savior, you can achieve anything. Accordingly, to his, God's will.

Everything is a process of steps. Taken the manifestation of God's love will flow through you.

Stand and affirm God's word.

God's truth, God's ways.

It is not our will be done, but God's will be done.

As I said, there are no mistakes we may do something that does not connect, or respond or does not match up to someone's standard, but we learn, we correct, we advance, so that is not a mistake.

Err, possibly, but do not ever condemn yourself or anyone else.

Setbacks are setups for a comeback. God has a purpose.

His ways and his light shine brightly.

Let it flow to you, through you and out into the hands and lives of others.

Nothing is Impossible......

Jeremiah 17-14 KJV Heal me, O Lod, and I shall be healed, save me, and I shall be saved. For thou art my praise.

Isaiah 40-31 NIV But those who hope in the Lord will renew their strength. They will soar on wings like eagles; they will run and not grow weary; they will walk and not faint.

Matthew 19-26 ESV But Jesus looked at them and said, "With man this is impossible, but with God all things are possible.

John 8-44 KJV "Ye are of your father the devil, and the lusts of your father ye will do. He was a murderer from the beginning, and abode not in the truth, because there is no truth in him. When he speaketh of his own; for he is a liar, and the father of it."

Micah 6-8 NIV He has shown you, O mortal, what is good, And what does the Lord require of you? To act justly and to love mercy and to walk humbly with your God.

John 3-16 KJV For God so loved the world, that he gave his only begotten Son, that whosoever believeth in him should not perish, but have everlasting life. **Luke 1-37 KJV** "For with God nothing shall be impossible."

Chapter 20

Everyone has an agenda.

Seems like you are lost and in an abyss. No one understands they are caught up in themselves, and it is all about themselves.

Hearing only their wants needs-God says he will meet our needs, and he does.

We are not responsible for someone who worships money, stuff, and themselves. We need to speak to them concerning God's love and his provisions.

As you are in and going through a loss, are in financial distress, <u>at the moment, at</u> a lack, look up to our creator.

Got to have it now, at this moment? God provides a way.

No matter what you are facing, <u>nothing</u> is critical to giving up on life, nor hope, nor trust and love of God.

There is nothing you can do on your own, alone, without the presence of the Father. You are not alone ever!

Finance/difficulties may arise. God will answer. There are other alternatives.

One may take out a loan, extend payment dates, employ/work towards, or even file bankruptcy, but to quit and lose hope is not an option at all to want, to quit.

Your today- your now- is a great gift from God.

Be grateful. Make a decision to: Rejoice in the Lord!

This shall pass.

Again, this shall pass. Wait patiently on the Lord.

Next, with so many people trying to impose their opinions as to why you won't succeed- or their opinions (interjections) of themselves, do not let it take hold of you- to where you see that image. Do not allow it.

You are someone-

Someone special and wonderfully made.

Thank the well-wishing, but do not let them become who God is. God's place is in your heart and alongside of you.

Hear God's word. Replace the thoughts with God's word.

Hurting and Crying Out

When Moses asked who you (name), he replied, (God) I am.

He is the great I am. Amazing, unique, and wonderful.

Let him make a difference in your life.

In context, you can know:

I am his child.

You can say:

I am his son or daughter.

I am a brother,

I am a sister,

I am a mother, I am a father.

I am made in the image of God.

I am someone who is loved.

It is so exhilarating to ride a dirt bike. I enjoy riding in the country. I do not do sugar bowls or jump mountains, but I do like free riding. In that, you can drive over the terrain feeling the wind blow and speed or not and hit a bump-up you go and <u>over</u>. A little bit more, go up, hit a big bump, go over, come down, you are making it. Then you see a curve, veer and turn, circling the course and returning safely. Ready for your next adventure?

Don't let anyone or anything rob you of that.

You have so much to give.

To your child or children.

Others that may be hurting too, can reach out to.

People who are in despair with health, being widowed, alone, etc.

You can make a difference in someone's life.

May you choose life and go on towards what God has called you to do.

There is no scale that registers (like Rictor for earthquakes) the pain you are in.

Be assured your reward is in heaven and God sees you. He knows you personally.

He registers every tear you weep.

God is faithful.

Know he has a plan and a future for you.

Embrace that and God's love for you.

It comes with no conditions,

God is not controlling. God is captivating.

The stories in the Bible are not from ancient times. They are relevant to today's times. A forewarning and direction come from God's word.

Let God reign in your heart speak to you right where you are.

Don't sit in the closet of darkness and believe lies and lose the wonderful life God has promised.

Seek him, knock, and he shall answer you. Make your requests known.

Believe in things yet to come. For it may only last a short time, but his love is forever.

His arms are open.

Come to him just as you are.

He will refine the broken pieces, and as beautiful as you already are, you will rise and shine much brighter.

Sooner than you ever even imagined.

God is hope, peace, love, and joy.

That's something to smile and sing about.

What we don't know, we can only just think about.

What we do know is God is real and stands on his words.

That's something to truly think about.

He loves you!

Psalm 68- 19 KJV Blessed be the Lord, who daily loadeth us with benefits, even the God of our salvation.

Hebrews 13-16 NIV And do not forget to do good and to share with others, for with such sacrifices God is pleased.

Psalm 27- 14 KJV Wait on the Lord: Be of good courage, and he shall strengthen thine heart, wait I say, on the Lord.

Colossians 3 23-24 ESV Whatever you do, work heartily, as for the Lord and not for men, knowing that from the Lord you, will receive the inheritance as your reward. You are serving the Lord Christ.

Jeremiah 18 4-6 KJV And the vessel that he made of clay was marred in the hand of the potter: so, he made it again another vessel, as seemed good to the potter to make it. Then the word of the Lord came to me, saying, O house of Israel, cannot I do with you as this potter? Saith the Lord, Behold, as the clay is in the potters' hand, so are ye in mine hand, O house of Israel.

Philippians 4-13 KJV "I can do all things through Christ which strengtheneth me."

Chapter 21

Do not be disillusioned by illusions.

Something you have concocted by thoughts and worry to build and grow.

Be a blessing to someone else who is either in the throes of what you are going through or have gone through.

Allowing the same from another. Open your arms to the same.

Seek wisdom.

Satan comes to deceive and destroy.

Using our weakness to interject his actions.

Jesus was tempted into many things, while he spent 40 days without even eating.

Jesus knows the things we will face as he experiences them.

God gives us enough grace not to quit.

To be strong in him.

Mercy, mercy!

You can do all things, call it out!

I can, I will, I shall!

Choose, no matter how difficult something or circumstances tend to be, to rest in thee. God our father. Releasing it unto him.

The almighty King of Kings, Lord of Lords.

If you take your mind and eyes off of yourself, you will find you are a blessing to someone else and much needed someplace else. We all are someone from someplace, we need one another.

The limitations placed can be removed with positive limits. Setting a goal for yourself and recognizing it.

Such as if you are unable to walk as freely as when you were younger. Gather a few friends together and circle the day with them. Each adds a special gift.

One may drive a few to go to breakfast or lunch, enjoy the talk and laughter, go help someone with making lunch or dinner, clean their house, share a short visit, and enjoy the gift of giving yourself to someone. Who does not have the means or the ability to do so? They will certainly enjoy it and you.

Hurting and Crying Out

Volunteer for a child's bible study. Sharing stories with the youth of today.

Paying for a night out for a couple that have a budget that won't allow them to afford it.

Kindness goes a long way.

God says, love your neighbors as yourself.

If you are feeling that things are too much, make an appointment with your doctor.

Possibly seek counseling.

Start seeing your church pastor.

All and everything- that leads to positive living and thinking. (The right mindset).

Maybe even take courses, listen to speakers, DVD's reading, or whatever it takes to activate the change of the thoughts.

Take a friend along. Go alone, become involved, and make new friends.

There is a season for everything.

God is in control, and he wants us all to be happy and to know that we are loved.

Being content in all things.

Depression is an impression created by circumstances we lack control of!

God has full power and control. Release it and surrender it unto him, and be free of the worry pounding down, it exists, and how you respond to it will make the difference.

The same with the right physician who can treat the symptoms and medicine may be very helpful.

God prepares us for all things.

God is with us in all things.

The power of prayer is moving and life-changing.

A smile quickly changes a frown and the atmosphere.

Start somewhere. Pull out that chair and get out of that; I don't care!

You are every bit worth it.

It does not matter what is going on or what you are currently in, you can when events such as death, illness, loss, divorce, children, or finances arise.

Turn immediately to the King.

Separate yourself from the inner turmoil and know, he not only has the answer, he God is the total answer.

I am the way, the truth, and the life.

Let God's light shine in and through you.

Take a breath-exhale.

For this moment-

Smile-as God is smiling down on you and with you.

He is a wonderful father.

Matthew 13-19 KJV When anyone hears the message about the kingdom and does not understand it, the evil one comes and snatches away what was sown in their heart. What was sown in their heart; This is the seed sown along the path.

Matthew 4 1-11 KJV Then Jesus was led by the Spirit into the wilderness to be tempted by the devil. After fasting for forty days and forty nights, he was hungry. The tempter came to him and said, "If you are the Son of God, tell these stones to become bread." Jesus answered, "It is written: Man shall not live on bread alone, but every word that comes from the mouth of God." Then the devil took him to the holy city and had him stand on the highest point of the temple: If you are the Son of God,: he said, throw yourself down;

For it is written: "He will command his angels concerning you, and they will lift their hands, so that you will not strike your foot against a stone." Jesus answered him: It is also written: Do not put the Lord your God to the test. Again, the devil took him to a very high mountain and showed him all the kingdoms of the world and their splendor. All this I will give you, he said," if you will bow down and worship me!" Jesus said to him, "Away from me, Satan!" For it is written: "Worship the Lord your God, and serve him only," Then the devil left him, and angels came and attended him.

2 Corinthians 12-9 NIV But he said to me, "My grace is sufficient for you, for my power is made in perfect weakness." Therefore, I will boast all the more gladly about my weaknesses, so that Christ's power may rest on me.

Leviticus 19-18 KJV Thou shalt not avenge nor bear any grudges against the children of thy people, but thou shalt love thy neighbor as thyself; I am the Lord.

Isaiah 45 6-7 NIV so that from the rising of the sun to the place of its setting people may know there is none besides me. I am the Lord, and there is no other. I form the light and create darkness, I bring prosperity and create disaster, I the Lord, do all these things.

Isaiah 62-10 KJV Go through, go through the gates; prepare ye the way of the people, cast up, cast up the highway; gather out the stones; lift up a standard for the people.

Psalm 144-15 KJV Happy is that people, that is in such a case yea. Happy is that people, whose God is the Lord.

Psalm 16 8-9 KJV "I have set the Lord always before me; because he is at my right hand, I shall not be moved." Therefore, my heart is glad, and my glory rejoiceth; my flesh shall rest in hope.

Chapter 22

I would like to promise you tomorrow will get better, but tomorrow is not here.

You have today and now.

Dreams are being answered, prayers are being answered. Good and wonderful things are now unfolding, love, smiles are on the horizon.

The defeat of yesterday is gone-

Joy camps in our souls- God is with us in us.

Rejoice!

This is the day; The Lord has made.

Embrace it.

You are closer than you think to better and greater.

How you feel emotions are not how God has provided, nor is it what he wants for you.

He supplies our needs daily.

God knows what they are.

God is not a rabbit's foot or a lucky charm.

The need for food, shelter, water outweighs the desire for a shiny new bike or car.

God knows all our needs and our desires.

God answers prayer.

Humble yourself and be grateful in and about all things.

Casting your care upon him.

Complaining is saying that you do not trust God.

You are not putting everything into his hands. You are putting buts, if I had, I would be happy, deals, whatever the case may be. God is our provider and God wants to richly bless us.

Everything belongs to God. God created it. So, God knows and is already at work providing.

Hurting and Crying Out

It may lead to more.

It may lead to where you have to take a step or steps to get there.

However, our father is a father indeed.

Regarding everything: goals, dreams, health, finances, necessities, children, family- Everything- God has got this!

You say God did not answer my prayer.

God does answer if it is his will.

"Thy will be done."

If it's obedient to the scriptures/God's word as God, it does not go against his word.

Some adversities make us stronger.

Some bring changes.

Some bring growth.

Some bring new horizons-dreams answered.

Some a rebirth-a renewal.

Don't question God as God is higher has created the universe and all under the sun.

Talk to God, converse with him, and tell him your concerns and wait for him to answer you.

You might want in your walk with God, when conversing, to ask if it is within his will and accordingly to his will, and God may provide you with the answer, direction, and the path which to take.

God is love, and God loves us unconditionally.

Seek ye the kingdom and all will be added to you.

Never stop praying.

Never stop seeking God.

The intimacy with God grows each and every day.

God is here for you.

It starts with you!

If you can make time for that television show (30 minutes to 60 minutes), you can surely shut it off and spend time with God. Same time spent on social media.

You will be glad you did.

People will let you down. People and their social media sites mean nothing.

If it is family and you are distant, yes, pictures mean something. However, your friends on a rock in Bermuda mean nothing. Enjoy it for them, but it really means nothing.

Build your relationship on the real rock!

The foundation of God.

You will be glad you did.

We are only passing through. The earth is not eternal. Heaven is. God is!

God's roads are paved in gold. God is golden.

Pure, lovely, magnificent.

Surpassing anything on or in this world.

Enjoy the relationship with God. Father, Son, and Holy Spirit. Indeed.

His love will shine out in your life, with your interactions in everything.

Joy will flow and peace which passes all understanding.

I used to say I would like to bottle and cap that feeling. It was amazing peace, and it does not need to be bottled. For He, God is with you. Always!

It is the peace the joy, that walking with God brings.

A peace and a joy that is always constant and always! God is love, peace, and joy.

Not things, not people.

We need to bring that love to others and show them through us-God's love.

Each and every one of us.

We have become fallen and shallow, ignoring, and snubbing one another and hurting people who need to know they are loved. God is a constant companion to all in need.

Call upon him.

Matthew 6-8 CEV Don't be like them. Your Father knows what you need before you even ask.

Jeremiah 29-12 NIV Then you will call on me and come and pray to me, and I will listen to you.

Isaiah 65 −24 KJV It will also come to pass that before they call, I will answer, and while they are speaking, I will hear.

1 Peter 5 6-7 ESV Humble yourselves, therefore, under the mighty hand of God so that at the proper time he may exalt you, casting all your anxieties on him, because he cares for you.

Psalm 106 25-26 NIV They grumbled in their tents and did not obey the Lord.

Romans 12-2 NIV Do not conform to the pattern of this world but be transformed by the renewing of your mind. Then you will be able to test and approve what God's will is-his good, pleasing and perfect will.

Ephesians 4-29 NIV Do not let any unwholesome talk come out of your mouths, but only what is helpful for building others up.

Deuteronomy 6-5 KJV "And thou shalt love the Lord thy God, with all thine heart, and with all thy soul, and with all thy might."

1 Samuel 22-23 NIV Stay with me; don't be afraid. The man who is trying to kill you is trying to kill me too. You will be safe with me.

Chapter 23

The manifestation of isolation limits your relationship with God.

When you limit God, you are placing holds on a wonderful relationship with God at his best.

God is constant.

God is love.

God is pure, wonderful, and elegant. Distinguished.

Kind and forgiving.

A source of all joy.

A companion, a father, continuous in everything.

Do not allow anyone to rob, steal, or kill your hope in God.

To take in your heart to receive Jesus as your savior.

There is not any time frame as to when you can receive Jesus. He is waiting for you.

Repent of your sins!

Invite Jesus into your heart and receive him as your personal savior.

He takes all of your sin/sins. He bore them on the cross.

You are forgiven.

You will live eternal life with him and not in Hades or as a non-believer. He, Jesus, sits on the right side of the Father. Amazing.

God so loved us, that he gave his Son Jesus, so that he who believes in him shall not perish, but have everlasting life.

That is such a wonderful and precious gift.

Would you not want it? To spend eternity with the creator of the universe?

A father so amazing?

Full of love?

The relationship you have with God is not the making of man or of earth.

It is unique because it is between you and God.

Father, Son, and Holy Spirit.

You are not lost but found.

Never to be alone.

God will never forsake you or leave you.

God is assurance.

Assurance of a life that is love.

Happiness, joy, peace, purity, soundness.

The Rock!

When someone says they do not believe, hold onto resurrection power, and let no one or anything tempt or sway you from the truth.

Endurance.

Run the race you were called for.

Being grateful for ALL things.

It does not matter what Frank thinks or what Chris believes. Sue may feel one way, and Mary feels another. We can lift each other and fellowship. Agree to disagree and even contest to the end, but with love and respect, we should- always love, forgive, and be willing to lead and show Christ through our hearts and actions and not allow anyone or anything to stand between our relationship with God.

God is constant. The same today as yesterday, the same tomorrow as today.

Never changing. Steadfast.

He is "I am".

He is the way.

He is the only true way.

Won't you commit to turning over your life to Jesus?

Repent and accept Christ as your personal savior?

Glorious is he indeed.

I mention this in several facets, where you may have overlooked the opportunity to invite/accept Jesus as your savior and now you may feel like receiving him as your savior.

Open your heart and surrender unto him.

God is!!

We are to encourage one another.

No one said we would sojourn through life by ourselves.

You can do nothing without God.

Nothing!

You did nothing alone or separate from Christ. He has been with you and by you always. As he is now.

When you wonder why no one asks, how are you doing? Do you ever ask God, how are you?

He has formed and created everything.

When seeking him, is it all about you, your wants?

Hurting and Crying Out

How about, Thank you!

How about, how are you?

How great you are Lord?

How about, how was your day?

Appreciation and adoration for our father. Father, Son, and Holy Spirit-I think you, yes, I thank you!

When you realize how great your creator is, you will see a manifestation of love, a power that is beautiful, and a master that is loving and kind.

King of Kings, Lord of Lords.

Our father.

Open up your heart and receive Christ as your savior.

His arms are always open.

His heart is never closed.

God loves you just how you are- no matter what the hour.

You will be glad that you did.

Count it all as joy.

Job 11- 7 NIV Can you fathom the mysteries of God? Can you probe the limits of the Almighty?

Psalm 18-2 NIV The Lord is my rock, my fortress and my deliverer; my God is my rock, in whom I take refuge, my shield and the horn of my salvation, my stronghold.

Hebrews 13 14-16 TLB For this world is not our home; we are looking forward to our everlasting home in heaven.

Revelation 3-20 KJV Behold, I stand at the door and knock: if any man hear my voice, and open the door, I will come in to him, and will sup with him, and he with me.

Romans 10-9 NIV If you declare with your mouth, "Jesus is Lord," and believe in your heart that God raised him from the dead, you will be saved.

Luke 15-24 KJV for this my son was dead, and is alive again; he was lost, and is found; And they began to merry.

Hebrews 12 13 NIV Therefore, since we are surrounded by such a great cloud of witnesses, let us throw off everything that hinders and the sin that so easily entangles.

And let us run with perseverance the race marked out for us, fixing our eyes on Jesus, the pioneer and perfector of faith.

For the joy set before him he endured the cross, scornina its shame, and sat down at the right hand of the throne of God. Consider him who endured such opposition from sinners, so that you will not grow weary and lose heart.

Lamentations 3 22-23 KJV It is of the Lord's mercies that we are not consumed because his compassions fail not.

They are new every morning great is thy faithfulness!

Psalm 100 4-5 NIV Enter his gates with thanksgiving and his courts with praise; give thanks to him and praise his name.

For the Lord is good and his love endures forever; his faithfulness continues through generations.

Chapter 24

Here(hear) and now? Appropriately phrased.

You are here and it is now! Have you heard the message from God?

He loves you.

In every form.

Your brokenness-

Hurting and Crying Out

It's affecting you totally.

You have arrived at this point (place) because God has spoken to you.

Age is a number not a definition.

Hearing the word and receiving God's word is the NOW, God wants you to hear and listen to.

You are someone and you do count.

No matter what transition, anxiety, or loss you are experiencing.

Nothing is too great or difficult for God.

Lost is not without hope or renewal.

Though you may feel as if time has stood still, you are in a dark tunnel; God promises rest for the weary.

No one, not even you, by trying to quit or give up will accomplish anything by such an action.

Stand and fight the good fight of faith.

Reassess these moments and rise above the occasion of angst to over-come the plight in front of you.

Let the weak say they are strong!

When Jesus bore our sins at and on the cross, he stood and rose again.

There is nothing, absolutely nothing, worth considering or attempting to take your life over. It is a gift, and you are a precious gift.

Jesus took everything on the cross for us, himself.

Certainly, let resurrection power engage you and speak and receive it in your heart.

A loss will get better, a divorce will mend and heal, a health diag-nosis will be handled and given strength by our creator. When you turn over everything and release it into the cup of Jesus' hands, he gives you the perfect balance to arrive where destiny has called you to be.

There is wisdom in numbers, seek it.

There is guidance for the shaken- seek them.

Counselors, family, pastoral groups/counseling, all and everything- that is causing you- so much angst- there is a door we can all use, that is God's door. Knock and I will answer, says the Lord.

Health illness, there are care providers, experts, surgeons. Seek out several opinions. There are options.

Pray/prayer continues communication with God.

Finances-nothing is too great for God.

Things happen- but there is bounce-back power.

God provides not only a way, but God provides the answer.

He is the way- The truth.

If you step away from yourself and your feelings.

You can feel the warmth of his love embracing you and know his love will also direct you in every fiber of current events.

There is no cause that you should feel so much in any way about quitting life.

Life is a gift.

God has many blessings we all have experienced and many more yet to come.

God's favor shines down on you and surrounds you.

How sweet it is to be loved by you. Yes, Lord, indeed.

For I know I am not alone, you are with me always!

Repeat the above and abound in God's love.

Hurting and Crying Out

You are with me always.

Recognize what you are facing- and in search of- let God restructure the building underway.

Do not let growth stagnate or hence stop production.

God created wonderfully masterpieces in each one of us.

As creator and designer of all he is there when you hit a wall, block, thunder.

Put on your hard hat and prepare for that skyscraper and rise to be you!

You are under construction.

Allow God to transform you.

And oh, what a beautiful transformation that you are.

As in building- permits, land, ideas, structure, etc. Take place to name a few.' In the essence of time, you are being renewed reborn.

It is hard to face many things in our lives that living life brings.

So, so many things are not our choosing, not our choices, not our faults, undeniably received, but we do not understand why- why me, Lord?

It is not you nor were you sought out. But you are strong, and God is our strength in all times, not just trying times.

God did not set out or did anything to destroy you, hurt you, or even place a thought in to quit inside us. He is a gentleman in every respect.

It is the enemy's actions to take what God has made for good.

To stop a whole loving relationship- adulating wholeheartedly and freely to God.

The enemy wants a foothold so you may join him in a journey and lifetime of hell. He can twist even the smallest thing to deceive you into believing and doubting.

The actions and given circumstances all fall into place with a course or direction of their own.

We may not want to lose someone in death. However, it was by natural calling was their time to come home unto God.

They also were ready and prepared for the entry of heaven and eternal life with God. Never hold anything against anyone. Forgive them no matter what.

Wanting someone to stay is natural. If it is a spouse, parent, child- but the physical pain they are experiencing is greater than the self of denying them or wanting that for them not to go and remain of selfish desires. Love has no holds and conditions. Love is letting go when times call for it. To love them enough that you want them out of pain and that they know they are loved and you love them.

We can do all things by Christ, who strengthens us. Everything that God has called us to do, we can, you can do. He would not have called you if it were not so.

As with cancer or some traumatic diagnosis, we do not want anyone to suffer unduly or because of our personal desires.

We should look up to God and let him lift us and fill us with his grace and his peace so we can be strong for them.

Enjoy and encourage one another.

Make each day special and special for them.

Today is the tomorrow you may not have.

Let them know you love them and you are there- for tomorrow put off, it will be or may not be their last day.

Everyone is a gift. Everyone is someone.

Embrace that, thank God for them, and the remembrance of each will always have a place in your heart and a light that shines inequitable by all shared uniquely with them.

Hurting and Crying Out

Placing your foot on the foundation of the Rock.

With all things release them unto God.

On bended knees come to him.

Brokenness, bow down to him, be humbled.

Glory, Glory, God almighty.

From the deepest of my heart, I pray that you will start.

Know you are special!

Know you are the righteousness of God.

There is absolutely nothing in this world worth giving your life up over or for.

Surrender your heart to God and know Jesus as your savior.

Things "WILL" fall into place.

You are chosen,

You are spoken for.

God has a plan for you.

Nothing is impossible for God or too big.

Our Father indeed.

Right now, tomorrow take, make the call for the help you need.

Let the Holy Spirit direct your steps.

Recognize who you are in Christ.

We are sons and daughters; we belong to a royal family.

King of Kings

Lord of Lords.

The only God.

1 John 4-19 KJV We love him, because he first loved us.

1 Peter 2-24 KJV Who his own self bore our sins in his own body on the tree, that we, being dead to sin, should live unto right-eousness, by whose stripes ye were healed.

1 Peter 5-7 NIV Cast all your anxiety on him because he cares for you.

Joel 3-10 KJV "Beat your plowshares into swords, and your pruninghooks into spears; let the weak say I am strong."

Numbers 6 24-26 NIV "The Lord bless you and keep you; the Lord make his face shine on you and be gracious to you; the Lord turn his face toward you and give you peace."

Matthew 28 −20 ESV Teaching them to observe all that I have commanded you.

And behold, I am with you always, to the end of the age.

Romans 12-2 KJV "And do not be conformed to this world, but be transformed by the renewing of your mind, that you may prove what is that good and acceptable and perfect will of God."

Romans 6-23 KJV "For the wages of sin(is) death; but the gift of God (is) eternal life through Jesus Christ our Lord."

Luke 21-28 KJV "And when these things begin to come to pass, then look up, and lift up your heads; for your redemption draweth nigh.

Philippians 2 9-11 NIV Therefore God exalted him to the highest place and gave him the name that is above every name, that at the name of Jesus every knee should bow, in heaven and on earth and under earth, and every tongue acknowledge that Jesus Christ is Lord, to the glory of God the father.

Chapter 25

You are a champion.

Hurting and Crying Out

No matter what you may have encountered, are going through, or even come up against, you will do it. Dare to believe. Receive. Know inside that you were created in the perfect image of God, and you are grand, a grand design.

You not only will do it, but you will master it.

Count on and rest in God and for all things.

We want to know control things, we want things the way we want things.

It is the NOW moment.

The right now moment.

The I want it now – I mean now moment.

Well, in the Lord, rest in him.

Not seeking your own, not threatening or demanding.

God is the way, the truth, and the life.

I do not know how

I do not understand- Why?

Why is all this happening to me?

Why, when I try so hard? It just keeps happening.

I can't take it anymore.

No one understands.

Wait- Yes, God understands.

He came in the image of man and went through all temptation before suffering on the cross for our sins.

Yes, the Holy Spirit resides in you and in me. The Holy Spirit will guide you and make intercession to God as we pray.

Christ having experienced and gone through temptations sits at the right side of God and expresses the temptations we all go through.

He, Christ, went through them and resisted.

God the Father, God the Son, God the Holy Spirit is everything.

Everything you or I will ever need.

Everything to know.

Sincere in all.

Loving and giving in all.

All sins are forgiven.

He is the answer.

He has the answers.

Sometimes, put yourself out there – to expect them to direct your steps and pray the battle within belongs to him.

The answers he will provide if they are his will and in accordance with his will.

Your future is planned with joy-so hope in God.

You can do all things through Christ who strengthens you.

I pray God bless you.

May you be a blessing to others.

May the hurt you are having and experiencing subside and you see God smiling down and on you.

May your today be bright

And your tomorrow be walking with God.

You will and you can.

The answers are all in God's hands.

In losses, accept God's hand and reign know that there are blessings in all things.

In the loss of a loved one or someone close.

Hurting and Crying Out

Know they are and always will be in your heart.

The love and all the times shared will always be special.

They will always be a part of you.

Thanking God for them and the time spent with them. A gift and special in every part.

Know they are out of pain, and they are with God, and be thankful!

They would want you to go on with your life and God does too.

God heals the brokenhearted and catches all and each of our tears in a bottle.

God is always nearby.

When it is too much God has and is carrying you,

You can let go and release all into God's mighty hands.

God hears you-

God answers you!

All beauty is a gift among many gifts given to you.

Receive it, them as such.

Count it all as joy!

God is the same today, yesterday, and tomorrow.

From generation to generation. God will be. God is, and you may call, come, invite, and know. He (God) is with you. God is for you. God will never abandon you or forsake you.

God provides all to us daily. God meets our needs and will see to it daily. Psalm 68:19

In accordance to thy kingdom come thy will be done. (The Lord's Prayer).

God's will.

You may be facing a health issue or a loved friend, whatever the case may be or who it may be.

God has no favorites. He loves us all unconditionally.

In health, God gives us promises, strength, hope, instruction, guidance.

Many regarding health.

By his stripes we are healed, it is one of many.

You are healed, place your name there and claim what God speaks.

Believe:

In your discouragement-

Hope, Don't doubt.

Believe!

Don't question.

Ask and you will receive.

Floundering back and forth is not trust.

Trust in him.

You are chosen-believe that!

Jeremiah 17:14

Heal me (your name), Oh Lord and I shall be healed,

Save me (your name), and I shall be saved.

For you are my praise.

Being joyful and joyful in all things.

It does not do the body good, loved ones, or anything to be miserable.

We each have something, and it is by sin in the garden. It was created by not obeying.

Hurting and Crying Out

We have God's promise of eternal life with him. He Jesus is the Living Water.

He died an excruciating death on the cross and bore all our sins.

Accept Jesus as your personal savior and know him.

God is with you.

God is for you.

In his (Jesus) suffering we were blessed. Even in ill health.

Be the child of God you were called to be.

Trust in him- That's the key.

Look up to him not a man not flesh.

You will see his love manifest.

When he says you can do all things.

Believe you can.

Take his hand.

He will be with you always.

My prayer is that you shall be healed.

May the blinders be replaced with hope assurance

That to the end of time, you can rest in him- and open your eyes to his promises.

It makes for no hope of bouncing up and down. Wishy, washy.

If God is the rock-

It is the foundation; it says he is solid.

It says he is strong-

Firm, concrete. It says you may rest in him.

He is our comforter.

Do it. Rest in him.

Hold firm and steady in our provider.

Rejoice in him and be thankful in all things. Truly grateful.

Tell everybody what a friend in Jesus we have.

Enjoy him, embrace him.

Share your joy.

Let the people around you know you love them.

Each day is a gift from God. Being the best you can be.

You are not alone. God is with you.

Even in loss illness.

You are not betrayed or left broken.

He (God) is there always in everything.

We are all given gifts, given time, be ye grateful and joyful, no matter.

Choose God-choose life.

Choose God's word and God's words. Always.

A word softly spoken is healing to the bones.

Love endures all.

God is love.

A wonderful and precious love.

Matthew 21-22 KJV And all things, whatsoever, ye shall ask in prayer, believing, ye shall receive.

Psalm 37-7 KJV Rest in the Lord and wait patiently for him; fret not thyself because of him who prospereth in his way, because of the man who bringeth wicked devices to pass.

Luke 11 9-10 NIV So I say to you; Ask and it will be given to you; seek and you will find; knock and the door will be opened to you. For everyone who asks receives; the one who seeks finds; and to the one who knocks, the door will be opened.

Isaiah 40-31 NIV But those who hope in the Lord will renew their strength. They will soar on wings like eagles; they will run and not grow weary; they will walk and not be faint.

Philippians 4 13 KJV I can do all things through Christ which strengtheneth me.

2 Peter 1-3 NIV His divine power has given us everything we need for a godly life through our knowledge of him who called us by his own glory and goodness.

John 5-15 NIV And if we know that he hears us- whatever we ask- we know that we have what we asked of him.

Corinthians 9-8 NIV And God is able to bless you abundantly, so that in all things at all times, having all that you need, you will abound in every good work.

Romans 12- 2 KJV And be not conformed to this world; but be ye transformed by the renewing of your mind, that ye may prove what is that good, and acceptable, and perfect, will of God.

Isaiah 46-4 NIV Even to your old age and gray hairs I am he, I am he, who will sustain you. I have made you and I will carry you; I will sustain you and I will rescue you.

Psalm 147-3 KJV He healeth the broken in heart, and bindeth up their wounds.

1 Thessalonians 5-23 KJV And the very God of peace sanctify you wholly; and I pray God your whole spirit and soul and body be preserved blameless unto the coming of our Lord Jesus Christ.

Isaiah 41-10 NIV So do not fear, for I am with you; do not be dismayed, for I am your God. I will strengthen you and help you; I will uphold you with my righteous right hand.

1 Peter 2-24 NIV "He himself bore our sins in his body on the cross so that we might die to sins and live for righteousness by his wounds you have been healed."

1 John 3-1 NIV See what great love the Father has lavished on us, that we should be called children of God! And that is what we are! The reason the world does not know us is that it did not know him.

Job 12-10 KJV In whose hand is the soul of every living thing, and the breath of all mankind.

1 Corinthians 13 7-8 ESV Love bears all things, believes all things, hopes all things, endures all things. Love never ends. As for prophecies, they will pass away; as for tongues, they will cease; as for knowledge, it will pass away.

Chapter 26

If it comes to finances, things, or goals, know that God is there.

There is nothing that you are facing that there is no an answer to.

Certainly, not money or possessions, stuff is any reason to quit, lose hope, or give up over.

Those things are idols.

Those things are about yourself and not anything you ever will take with you.

In eternal life, there is a road paved with gold. God is beyond what worldly possessions are and any meaning attached to them.

God supplies all our needs.

Things are gifts provided by God and all belong to God.

Hope and trust in him.

Being grateful for everything.

Pray about it.

Hurting and Crying Out

Pray over it.

In everything, come to him, come before him, and ask.

He does not want you broken, frozen, empty, and hurting.

He says you have not because you ask not.

Seek

Knock

Ask

Put yourself aside and pray to God in and about all things.

Seeking God first in all things.

God wants to give you the desires of your heart.

When you are faced with adversity go to your father and ask.

Make your requests known.

He will answer- He will provide- He is the answer!

He is the bread of Life.

Reverence for God, Respect, and love.

The earth has many obstacles and believers of all kinds.

The believer that does in himself, by himself-

False! God says: We can do nothing apart (absent) from God.

The believer of things, money, possessions are idols.

God supplies all our needs.

Let not anything become an idol.

God is our creator.

There is nothing that you are facing that has not been before and overcome in most. You are not the first nor will you be the last. No, it is not easy. Yes, it does hurt.

God says do not become unequally yoked.

Do not put yourself in a position that goes against the will of God.

God says take hold of him. His burden is light. God is not stressed out or broken down.

Together you can do all things.

You are not alone, and you never will be alone.

There is no difference between white or black, rich or poor. We are all children of God.

We belong to the heavenly kingdom and a family in and with Father, Son, and Holy Spirit.

In heaven there is no religion.

The Lord God Almighty and the Lamb are its temple. Revelation 21;22. We are the temple of God.

Reverence and joy we shall encounter and outpour to preach and show one another the love of God. The love of Christ.

All things are a gift.

Count it all as joy.

In all things-Rejoice!

You shall overcome the obstacles you are experiencing and choose to believe they are obstacles.

They may appear large, but they are not. There is nothing that God can't provide.

God is greater!

Lean into God's understanding.

Change the things you can- Always with praise and thanksgiving.

May God's grace be received so you may be able to achieve the things God has bestowed on you to complete.

Hurting and Crying Out

God is with you always in all things.

It is a battle going on daily. Pray, pray and pray.

You are a warrior to God's victorious creation. He made you in his own image.

God spoke-

God made-

God says-

Worship your father.

Love your father unconditionally.

Know Jesus as your savior.

The course race you are set to accomplish. It has been designed specifically for you.

Several factors:

Race a word does not mean that it is a race per se. You quickly must accomplish, nor is it you!

God has a future, a plan for all of us.

We also have choices.

Some of those choices may be good or not, but some may go against the course that was designed.

God says to choose wisely.

It becomes overwhelming when we don't have all the answers.

It becomes angst when our need to control should be to Let Go!

Self goes nowhere.

A perpetual cycle of circles and unhappiness.

We need each other- not to use each other.

More so God first.

Turning to God in everything.

He does not want part of you, he wants all of you.

Guard your heart and watch over your mind.

Feelings and emotions come and change daily hourly. Release the negative and pick a positive.

Step by step, you can achieve the reframing of your thoughts.

His ways are higher than our ways!

God says come to me who are weary, and I (God) will give you rest.

Right now, change begins with releasing God's word- and not being in control.

Self is given a new revision in becoming Christ-driven.

Pure, lovely. And noble.

Your answer will come, and you shall arrive.

Be patient in all things.

Everything has its purpose.

Everything has its appointed timing.

Allow, receive God into your whole life and be, watchful to his will and by his will- it shall be done.

Matthew 28-20 KJV Teaching them to Observe all things whatsoever I have commanded you; and, lo, I am with you always even unto the end of the world. Amen.

Genesis 1 1-2 NIV In the beginning God created the heavens and the earth. Now the earth was formless and empty, darkness was over the surface of the deep, and the spirit of God was hovering over the waters.

2 Corinthians 6 –14 KJV Be ye unequally yoked together with unbelievers: for what fellowship hath righteousness with unrighteousness? And what communion hath light with darkness?

John 16-32 KJV: Behold, the hour comet, yea, is now come, that ye shall be scattered, every man to his own, and shall leave me alone: And yet I am not alone, because the Father is with me.

Philippians 3 2021 NIV But our citizenship is in heaven. And we eagerly await a Savior from there, the Lord Jesus Christ. Who by the power that enables him to bring everything under his control, will transform our lowly bodies so that they will be like his glorious body.

2 Timothy 3-14 NIV But as for you, continue in what you have learned and have become convinced of, because you know those from whom you learned it.

Isaiah 45-22 NIV "Turn to me and be saved all you ends of the earth; for I am God, and there is no other."

John 1-12 KJV But as many as received him, to them gave He power to become the sons of God, even to them that believe on his name.

Chapter 27

We are all unique and different.

What bothers you does not bother me and vice versa.

That is where we can lift one another.

We are approved by God and are his children.

You must step aside and breathe in what God has called you to do.

Be strong and of good courage.

It may look impossible: one event right after another, as if a train is coming at you. A loss here, a call there, someone ill - maybe even you. All of a sudden, it is one thing right after the other.

Do not be afraid or intimidated.

You will be ok!

Better than ok too!

Take each event and receive and process it.

God is with you.

There is a positive in the negative.

Prevention is an introduction to the invention.

The invention is the new you.

A new you,

A stronger you, A better you.

Success is on its way.

You can bring it.

God is with you and for you.

The turbulence is only temporary and though clouds may appear, and you are thrown this way and that-

A calm and new start is always evident in the forthcoming moments.

Allow yourself to embrace yourself.

Not maybe being as you envisioned- your dreams, your goals, maybe even greater than you imagined.

Allow the creation to unveil what God has created and designed for you.

If God is for you, who dare be against you?

Hurting and Crying Out

The limitations "you" set for yourself, you must not be anxious for nothing.

In all things, acknowledge Him, God, and he will see you through.

A setback is a set-up for a comeback.

You have bounce-back power.

Hope, believe, and know God has you in the palm of his hand.

Don't quit- don't allow excuses to stop you from being who God has called you to be.

God's love is unconditional.

If for a moment-

Now-

Remember a time, a place-

You know-

You went-

It had beauty, peace, calm, joy- you loved it!

We all have one.

It sets you in a state of joy and tranquility.

So, there it is. Embrace this moment, now.

A waterfall sitting quietly by the stream and watching it quietly cascade into the cove. The beauty God has created is evident. Birds singing feet dangling in the cool water smiling.

One canoeing down the river, quietly seeing the way of the course, you are steering in the right direction, enjoying the trip alone, or with someone else.

A birthday party- friends, family, laughter, all enjoying a wonderful day-

Your first kiss- a walk with your partner-

The positive, happy, and serene moments times we have, we go there and bring that special moment.

Response is the correct manner in what is important.

Nothing is ever too difficult that you cannot do or accomplish.

Foremost remember that

And God loves you!

God is-

God is first! Always!

Whatever you are facing, he is there, go to him.

Seek him.

For everyone needs someone they can talk to laugh with, someone they can enjoy, who wants nothing in return.

We are all someone- Be that somebody to another.

Right now, people appear as takers. Fakes, imposters, posers-

They are unhappy-

Lacking joy-lacking love and connections-

"Don't" let that stop you from doing and being who God has chosen you to be.

Rest in him.

Totally believe in God

Assured by faith- All things work together for the good of those who love him.

He is the answer.

Take your questions to him.

Cry out to him- Pour out to him-

Watch God prevail in your storms.

Hurting and Crying Out

Do <u>not</u> let <u>any</u> weapon formed against you prosper!

It is clearly defined <u>no</u> weapon formed shall prosper.

Next, direct your steps, your course, so shall it be on the path he, God, has placed you.

Taking nothing for granted.

Even in the hurt, pain, affliction, loss, circumstances.

Turn to surrender into God's hands all pertaining to, get prosper counsel, consult with professionals, separate evil tendencies to the proper and true channels of life flowing and living waters.

As the saying goes-

How sweet it is to be loved by you!

Wrap yourself around in God's love and God's ways.

The people you cut loose and separate from, pray for them.

The people who hurt you, cover them. The people no longer here- accept it-honor it- and pray.

Pray for strength understanding and God shall supply all your needs!

God is concrete, Solid. Solid as the Rock!

Same yesterday, tomorrow, and today. Forever more.

Let love flow when all things have walls or you are hitting walls. Smile when all is lost or broken- hug when all is turned and not receptive- believe when eyes are closed- love when the heart feels torn and broken.

You shall rise again, let no occasion stop you from believing the beautiful words of God, softly spoken.

They were spoken for you and about you!

God is love.

There is no other feeling, deep emotion, than the love of God and the love we have and can have for God. A very intimate and deep everlasting relationship that never fails.

I will repeat it again: How sweet it is to be loved by you!

Romans 13-1 KJV "Let every soul be subject unto the higher powers. For there is powers that be ordained by God."

John 13 34-35 NIV A new commandment I give to you, that you love one another; just as I have loved you, you also are to love one another. By this all people will know that you are my disciples, if you have love for one another.

Romans 13-1 KJV "Let every soul be subject unto the higher powers. For there is no power but of God: the powers that be ordained of God."

John 13 34-35 NIV A new commandment I give to you, that you love one another; just as I have loved you, you also are to love one another. By this all people will know that you are my disciples, if you have love for one another.

2 Timothy 2-15 NIV Do your best to present yourself to God as one approved, a worker who does not need to be ashamed and who correctly handles the word of truth.

Romans 12-11 NIV Never be lacking in zeal but keep your spiritual fire or serving the Lord.

Colossians 3 1-4 NIV Since then, you have been raised with Christ, set your hearts on things above, where Christ is, seated at the right hand of God. Set your mind on things above, not on earthly things. For you died, and your life is now hidden with Christ in God. When Christ, who is your life, appears, then you also will appear with him in Glory.

Romans 8 26-28 NIV We do not know what we ought to pray for, but the Spirit himself intercedes for us through wordless groans. And he who searches our hearts knows the mind of the Spirit, because the Spirit intercedes for God's people in accordance with the will of God.

Malachi 3-6 NIV "I the Lord do not change. So, you, the descendants of Jacob, are not destroyed."

Chapter 28

Life is not simple and has complications.

From missing a bus or an appointment.

From a broken finger to a broken heart.

We receive things differently.

Such is the loss of a partner. Some say he or she, the love of their life is totally stricken. Love is deep. Others say, get over it.

Finances cut corners regroup, others totally abound in brokenness.

Times and events lead us to many feelings or emotions- But we have no control over the future.

We can choose to be joyful in all things.

Even the most heart-wrenching things as God will lead us in and through them.

God does not want us to hurt. Satan uses our weaknesses so he can overcome our devotion and love for God. To distance us from the love and calling that God has for each one of us.

Sometimes, it is testing.

We need to be stronger, giving more love and to ourselves even when things are not going our way.

Be strong in the Lord.

People will hurt you and sometimes there are no answers or understanding, but God knows. God cares and he sees your hurt. He has prepared a table. Sit down and eat with him.

Rest, give it, pray about and over it.

Totally releasing it into unto him.

Then watch

The mending begins- you are healed- you find peace- rest and love, what was bothering you no longer matters- it was not even impor- tant when it started- now just a small thought- let the time you have be that of advancement of kindness – a child of God.

No longer let anything make you distraught or placed in despair.

Claim the word of God powerful in the movement and life of all things.

Greater is he that is in you than in the world.

Passion is Christ.

Live your passion.

Dare to dream-

Dream big-

Let your dream be a reality.

Don't be a statistic as a result of another's meaningless attempt to belittle you.

There is no reason to ever feel less than when God is more than and greater than.

Takes the likes off of social media. Who cares?

Take the comments off- Really, does it mean anything?

Some people you will never please.

This person, that person, are they going to be a foundational and lasting part of your life?

They do not like this or that and say this and that.

Do they do the work?

Hurting and Crying Out

Do they know you?

Does it matter??

Have they prepared you as God has? You are this and you are that, really?

How about you are a child of God, and you have a calling and a purpose??

You are diagnosed with an illness- can you treat, overcome, and know God has this.

It's ok to be scared-

It's ok to cry

It's ok to hurt.

Let God heal the hurt.

Jesus nailed to the cross, thorns in his head, pierced, and gouged horribly.

Sweating blood.

We can overcome because he did.

His power, love, and peace of healing has all been passed onto you.

You are forgiven-

You are healed-

Nothing, no weapon, formed against you shall prosper.

Hence, if Jesus paid the price of all our sins, who are we to decide?

Who are we who want our own way to question anything?

Jesus came, Jesus knew, and Jesus has gone through (yes, gone through) knows every temptation, every hurt, and in hanging on the cross, said Father, forgive them, for they know not what they do.

Amazing-

A declaration of the most humanly selfless love ever imaginable.

So, as Jesus did And

Jesus sits at the right side of God-

And the Holy Spirit is in us as individuals making intercession on our behalf- How great is that?

Think a moment

Three (3) parts-

You have watched over you and with you always- knowingly. Surrender yourself into the hands of - and watch them do something amazing in your life.

Many things come crop up, pop up, in our lives.

Some are easier than others-

Some are easier for others than for you, but we are uniquely made. Each and every one of us is different.

It is always nice to have someone at your side to lift you, but let Christ be your source.

Go to your bible-

Search daily scriptures (the word and truth of God).

God spoken-

Pain is in and comes in many forms.

God is our healer- Believe in God's words.

Heal me and I am healed.

Save me and I am saved.

Praise God.

He will not only lead you, but He, God, will provide.

Provide surgeons, doctors, answers.

Hurting and Crying Out

"Comfort".

Yes, comfort.

He is our comforter in all things.

If you ask, you shall receive.

Seek wisdom in what you Can't.

God Can!!

A loss-

Whether friends, family, enemies, whatever be

Count it all, joy

Yes, my love, count it all joy.

It was a gift

A treasure.

These moments are always forever.

Maybe you cared more than i.e., Marriage, partner, friends, enemy, family that's why it hurts, and it is painful.

However, they were not meant by God to be in your life

God has another plan designed for you.

Open your eyes, your heart, and your arms to welcome what God has in store-

And walk through that door not challenged but with the challenge God has for you specifically.

Do not be weighed down by the world and absorbed in it.

Absorption is a word that sucks, holds, and in that you can be drawn away by the lust of the flesh.

Welcome the Center of the Universe (God created all), and welcome love, being grounded, and being sound in Christ.

You will see the vision he has and your vision of entwining themselves into something very beautiful.

The key to happiness is the decision to be happy. Not searching around for it. To know God and to love God is happiness beyond ever imagined.

God is constant solid. True, noble, lovely, pure, amazing, everything that you or I will ever need. Emulate the traits of God. All others are to be added and should be viewed as treasures.

You are a treasure.

God loves you.

Seek his way, his will.

Welcome him into your heart.

Today, right now, open your heart.

Make a new start.

Envision your dreams, your hopes, and your goals coming true.

Wait eagerly upon him (God) to answer and show you.

Do not demand your own.

Contest the best.

Call out and you are blessed.

Let God do the rest!

You can-

You will be who God has certainly called you to be

If you don't quit.

If you let God shoulder all of your pain- If... you let God....

If you surrender your life to Jesus.

Proverbs 3-5 KJV "Trust in the Lord with all thine heart; and lean not unto thine own understanding."

Psalm 56-4 KJV In God I will praise his word, In God I have put my trust; I will not fear what flesh can do unto me.

Galatians 5-24 KJV And they that are Christ's have crucified the flesh with the afflictions and lusts. If we live in the Spirit, let us also walk in the spirit.

Psalm 147 3 KJV He healeth the broken in heart, and bindeth up their wounds.

Hebrews 4-15 KJV "For we have not an high priest which cannot be touched with the feeling of our infirmities; but was in all points tempted like as we are, yet without sin."

Joshua 1-8 NIV Keep this Book of the Law always on your lips; meditate on it day and night, so that you may be careful to do everything written in it.

Matthew 28-19 KJV Go ye therefore, and teach all nations, baptizing them in the name of the Father, and the Son, and of the Holy Ghost.

Amos 5-14 KJV Seek good, and not evil, that ye may live; and so, the Lord, the God of hosts shall be with you, as ye have spoken.

Malachi 3-6 NIV "I the Lord do not change. So, you, the descendants of Jacob, are not destroyed."

1 Corinthians 13-5 KJV Doth not behave itself unseemly, seeketh not her own, is not easily provoked, thinketh no evil.

Chapter 29

Open that door, the window of hope and let God's light shine in.

He will fill the loneliness.

He will heal the ill.

He will open the eyes of shades of darkness.

He will heal the hearts of the broken.

He will supply your needs.

He will bring people into your life.

God is hope.

God is eternal.

God is constant and always true.

Full of love, compassion, and grace.

You too can excel in beating what has a hold of you, what is weighing you down, what thoughts are popping up.

Ask God and you shall see-

That God is there for you and me.

Words have an impact.

Speak God's word over yourself, imparting to whereas the promises are spoken for you.

There are difficulties in life, this is true.

There are days worse than others- but it doesn't have to be so.

We can find joy in it and all circumstances and events.

We can Rejoice in the Lord!

We can sing and have a new song in our hearts.

We must make a start.

Turning and surrendering yourself to Jesus-

Turning over your heart.

Everything that you do counts as a victory.

Don't lose you-

Hurting and Crying Out

Don't quit-

You are reading this book, and we are just people in the end.

Someone from somewhere.

But what we all have in common is we are the children of God in the same family.

That, my love, screams something!

You count-

Your voice counts-You mean something-

You are valuable-

You are talented-

You are loved and you are treasured.

Let no weapon formed against you prosper, no, no weapon.

With what comes against, God is the answer, and there is light at the end of the tunnel.

No one asked you to go it alone and you don't. God is with you always from the beginning to the end.

Greater is he that is in you than in this world.

Saying that hurting people hurt others.

Let this not be true of you.

Know God's promises and stand on them.

Overcome what you are facing, as it is you are facing, do not let it overcome you or even welcome it. Refuse to entertain it. Allow the Holy Spirit to guide you.

Don't be taken suckered by the moment or by a feeling or an emotion.

Be the person and all that God has called you to be. Step out.

The today you experienced is now just a memory- your tomorrow is on the horizon- let hope come in joy bubble from your heart- And speak I can, I will, and I am!

You most certainly will.

Let no one or anything deceive you.

What has entered is trying to deceive you to quit. Do not allow it entrance, show it the door. Be the master of your temple and allow God to flow through.

You are an achiever.

Dream big! Dream Big! As Christ Reigns!

John 14-27 NIV "Peace I leave with you, my peace I give unto you. Not as the world giveth, give I unto you. Let not your heart be troubled, neither let it be afraid."

Hebrews 13-5 NIV Keep your lives free from the love of money and be content with what you have, because God has said, "Never will I leave you; never will I forsake you."

3 John 1-2 KJV Beloved, I wish above all things that thou mayest prosper and be in health, even as thy soul prospereth.

Acts 26-18 NIV To open their eyes and turn them from darkness to light, and from the power of Satan to God, so that they may receive forgiveness of sins and a place among those who are sanctified by faith in me.

Philippians 4-19 ESV And my God will supply every need of yours according to his riches in glory in Christ Jesus.

Revelation 17-14 KJV They shall make war with the lamb and the Lamb shall overcome them: for he is Lord of lords, and Kings of Kings: and they that are with him are called, and chosen, and faithful.

Job 8-19 KJV Behold, this is the joy of his way, and out of the earth shall others grow.

Philippians 4-4 KJV Rejoice in the Lord always; and again, I say, Rejoice.

John 3-16 KJV For God so loved the world, that he gave, his only begotten Son, that whosoever believeth in him should not perish, but have everlasting life.

Isaiah 43- 4 ESV Because you are precious in my eyes, and honored, and I love you; I give men in return for you, peoples in exchange for your life.

Isaiah 54-17 KJV No weapon that is formed against shall prosper and every tongue that shall rise against thee in judgment thou shalt condemn. This is the heritage of the servants of the Lord, and their righteousness is of me, saith the Lord.

1 John 4-4 NIV You dear children are from God and have overcome them, because the one who is in you is greater than the one who is in the world.

Psalm 46-1 NIV A song, God is our refuge and strength, an ever-present help in trouble. There is a river whose streams make glad the city of God, the holy place where the Most High dwells. God is within her; she will not fall; God will help her at break of day.

1 Peter 5-10 NIV And the God of all grace, who called you to his eternal glory in Christ, after you have suffered a little while, will himself restore you and make you strong, firm and steadfast.

1 John 4-4 NIV You dear children, are from God and have overcome them, because the one who is in you is greater than the one who is in the world.

James 1-12 KJV Blessed is the man that endureth temptation; for when he is tried, he shall receive the crown of life, which the Lord hath promised to them that love him.

Chapter 30

Counseling is available.

All things take steps and actions. Positive actions.

Make the calls today to break down those walls, the strongholds from hindering you from being the best God has created.

We can all come up with excuses.

We can all put stoppers at our doors.

Dare to open that door and walk through to a brighter and better you.

You may stumble and even fall, but God is with you every step of the way and in every moment.

If God is for you- who dare go against you?

It is a process-

Make up your mind to do it and let the transformation begin.

We are never too old to do anything or to be bold.

Age is only a number; factors are predicated by God and God's plans for you.

You can do all things through Christ who strengthens you!

Yes, all things.

If God has declared it, you declare he is the source, take the course.

Direct yourself into his leadership and direction.

Master, a creator, our father.

It was foretold many years before it happened Christ, being born and the crucifixion. Psalms 22 talks about it and also Isaiah.

Hurting and Crying Out

God's word is the doctrine and how we should go about and live. A book that goes and lasts/lives through the times and from the end of time, from generation to generation. The Bible, the Holy word.

"Live" the life you have not only been designed to live and also chosen to live and enjoy but enjoy every moment of it.

Even the trials, the sorrows, the pain, it all has meaning, count it all as joy.

God is with you and God is for you.

God will never give you more than you can bear or carry.

God sees you as strong, even when you feel you are not.

If God knows this how on earth could he be wrong?

He created everything. Clouds, grass, birds, water, the entire universe, therefore, what you are feeling and facing, he can't create an answer or a calm?

Of course, God can. God calms the storms, the wind, and God can make all things possible. Believe and trust in God. Turning it all over to him. Waiting upon his will, his timing, and in his timing. Be of good courage.

Rest in him. Submit all into his hands (not yours) and wait for his answer (not yours).

He knows the cries of his children; he hears us all.

Stand up!

Stand up and shout your cry for help. Your need to God.

Bring your pain and troubles to him.

Shout- Shout them out.

He will welcome you, shelter you, and answer you!

Whatever obstacle that or obstructs stacked (multiple), let God hold them. Not you. Release the stress of trying to do everything. Release them.

Release the torment.

Let God heal you, walk with you, guide you, and be the one you hear.

What you are facing, be of good cheer as God is the answer.

Right now, <u>start</u> taking the steps for success, breaking chains holds on you. Start renewing your mind with a right and positive mindset.

Each step, each thought is a step to be your best and what God has created.

You are the best!

Always remember that.

Don't give up!

Don't quit!

It is God who equips each of us.

Put on the whole armor of God and be the beautiful person you are designed and was designed to be. Today and forever more- You are loved!

Ephesians 6-12 KJV "For we wrestle not against flesh and blood, but against principalities, against the rulers of darkness of this world, against spiritual wickedness in high places."

Philippians 4-13 KJV "I can do all things through Christ which strengthens me."

1 Kings 8-56 KJV "Blessed be the Lord, that hath given rest unto his people Israel, according to all that he promised; there hath not failed one word of all his good promises, which he promised by the hand of Moses his servant."

Isaiah 41-10 NIV "So do not fear, for I am with you; do not be dismayed, for I am your God."

Corinthians 10-13 NIV But you can trust God. He will not let you be tempted more than you can bear. But when you are tempted, God will also give you a way to escape that temptation.

Ephesians 6-10 KJV Finally, my brethren, be strong in the Lord, and in the power of his might.

Timothy 2-1 KJV Thou therefore, my son, be strong in the grace that is in Christ Jesus.

2 Timothy 3-16 ESV All scripture is breathed out by God and profitable for teaching and reproof, for correction, and for training in righteousness.

Mark 11-24 ESV Therefore I tell you, whatever you ask in prayer, believe that you have received it, and it will be yours.

Conclusion

Every day we are met with struggles.

God did not intend for us to be broken and hurting.

Jesus came and died for our sins.

The worldly things of this passing/sojourning are a direct path, we have been designed for. God says-speaks.

I have a future for "YOU". Full of hope. -Plans.

God wants us to hear him-know him.

There are many obstacles, events, angst, hate, dislike, evil, out there. We are strong in and by Christ. In and by God the Father.

Please stop and do NOT allow anything or anyone to hold you. Own you. Prevent you. Hinder you. Ridicule you.

You are valuable and important.

Beautiful and unique.

Presented with many talents and gifts!!

Do not lose sight of what God holds dear and that is YOU!

You are so wanted and needed.

Yes-

Stand and Shout!

You are somebody- you are precious and who God says you are!

Live to love and be loved.

Live to be who God has called you to be.

You are wonderful!

www.ingramcontent.com/pod-product-compliance
Lightning Source LLC
Chambersburg PA
CBHW051445130726
47987CB00005B/2195